PRIVATE RIGHTS, PUBLIC PROBLEMS

A guide to NAFTA's controversial chapter on investor rights

IISD INTERNATIONAL INSTITUTE FOR
SUSTAINABLE DEVELOPMENT
INSTITUT INTERNATIONAL DU
DÉVELOPPEMENT DURABLE

WWF

Copies are available from IISD.
Copies may also be ordered through IISD's online order form at
<http://iisd.ca/about/prodcat/ordering.htm>.

National Library of Canada Cataloguing in Publication Data

Main entry under title:

Private rights, public problems

Published in association with: World Wildlife Fund.
ISBN 1-895536-39-1

1. Canada. Treaties, etc. 1992 Oct. 7. Chapter 11.
2. Free trade—Environmental aspects—North America.
3. Investments, Foreign—Law and legislation—North
America. I. International Institute for Sustainable
Development. II. World Wildlife Fund

HF1746.P75 2001   382'.917   C2001-910528-2

This publication is printed on recycled paper.

International Institute for Sustainable Development
161 Portage Avenue East, 6th Floor
Winnipeg, Manitoba CANADA
R3B 0Y4

Tel: (204) 958-7700
Fax: (204) 958-7710
E-mail: info@iisd.ca
Internet: http://www.iisd.org

Table of Contents

**Private Rights,
Public Problems:**
A guide to
NAFTA's
controversial
chapter on
investor rights

International Institute for Sustainable Development

IISD's vision is better living for all—sustainably; its mission is to champion innovation, enabling societies to live sustainably. It is an independent, not-for-profit corporation headquartered in Winnipeg, Canada, established and supported by the governments of Canada and Manitoba.

IISD's Trade and Investment work has been ongoing since 1991. In that time it has continuously worked to broaden the focus of the debates from trade and environment to trade and sustainable development, to incorporate the essential concerns of developing countries. It aims to promote solutions that will help trade and investment contribute to the broad objectives of sustainable development.

It has published widely, on topics including WTO reform, MEAs, trade-related intellectual property rights, investment rules, science and precaution, international environmental management and western hemispheric integration. This book is the product of IISD's Investment Law and Sustainable Development Project.

For more information, visit IISD's web site at http://www.iisd.org.

World Wildlife Fund (WWF-U.S.)

Known worldwide by its panda logo, World Wildlife Fund (WWF) is dedicated to protecting the world's wildlife and wildlands. The largest privately-supported international conservation organization in the world, WWF has nearly five million members worldwide (more than one million in the U.S. alone). Since its inception in 1961, WWF has invested in over 13,100 projects in 157 countries. WWF directs its conservation efforts toward three global goals: protecting endangered spaces, saving endangered species and addressing global threats. From working to save the giant panda, tiger and rhino to helping establish and manage parks and reserves worldwide, WWF has been a conservation leader for more than 39 years.

WWF's Sustainable Commerce Program is dedicated to promoting conservation through engagement with public policy issues surrounding trade, investment and international commerce. The Program's objective is to help create the laws, policies and processes needed to make international commerce sustainable in both human and ecological terms.

For more information, please visit WWF at http://www.worldwildlife.org.

Preface

Private Rights,
Public Problems:
A guide to
NAFTA's
controversial
chapter on
investor rights

*Their meetings are secret. Their members are generally
unknown. The decisions they reach need not be fully disclosed.
Yet the way a small group of international tribunals handles
disputes between investors and foreign governments has led to
national laws being revoked, justice systems questioned and
environmental regulations challenged. And it is all in the name
of protecting the rights of foreign investors under the North
American Free Trade Agreement.*

— *New York Times*
March 11, 2001

For those concerned with sustainable development and the
conservation of our planet's living resources, international
efforts to promote "foreign direct investment" must be at once
a source of hope and of concern. On one hand, the economic
growth that foreign investment can stimulate in countries
where poverty is a leading cause of human suffering and
environmental degradation is a necessary ingredient of
sustainable development. Without growing international
investment, we would all face a diminished future.

On the other hand, international investment and the rules
and institutions that encourage it can—and in some cases
do—pose a threat to sustainable development. Simply
increasing investment is not enough to guarantee that new
wealth will be distributed equitably, or that rising commerce
will be based on environmentally sound activities. For
international investment to contribute to achieving
development that is sustainable, governments will have to
continue helping set the legal and economic context in which
investment takes place.

It is, therefore, ironic that some of the new international
mechanisms designed to encourage foreign direct investment
have themselves begun to interfere with this vital
governmental role. Nowhere is this more evident than in the
growing experience under the investment rules contained in
Chapter 11 of the North American Free Trade Agreement
(NAFTA)—the subject of this guide. In the seven years since
NAFTA's entry into force on January 1, 1994, multinational
corporations have used Chapter 11 to challenge a raft of
public regulations in all three NAFTA countries: Canada, the
United States and Mexico. Particularly disturbing is the large
proportion of these cases that are brought against
environmental laws and regulations.

**Private Rights,
Public Problems:**
A guide to
NAFTA's
controversial
chapter on
investor rights

While challenges to government actions are inevitably part of
providing legal protection for foreign investors, the
implementation of Chapter 11 to date reflects a disturbing
lack of balance between the protection of private interests and
the need to promote and protect the public welfare. The
nature of the challenges brought so far has even surprised
many of the agreement's authors. As this guide went to press,
there were signs from the Canadian and Mexican
governments of a growing readiness for reform. The
government of the United States, meanwhile, has quietly
undergone more than two years of sharp and unresolved
internal debate over the direction of U.S. international
investment policy.

Whether the problems under Chapter 11 are a matter of
"unintended consequences" or reflect a more profound
imbalance in NAFTA's approach, they remain real. But despite
the history of Chapter 11—and despite the dramatic failure in
1998 of negotiations aimed at a global agreement
incorporating many of Chapter 11's salient features—
NAFTA's investment rules continue to provide the working
model for the proposed Free Trade Area of the Americas, and
for other international agreements.

Some observers consider criticisms of Chapter 11 premature,
arguing that the case law under NAFTA is still in early
development. But the stakes are too high, the problems too
evident and the trends in the jurisprudence too disturbing to
allow complacency. This guide is aimed at helping the general
public understand the elements of the debate over Chapter
11. It is intended to provide a simple, up-to-date reference
point that will allow its readers to contribute to a well-
informed discussion of the future of NAFTA and other
international investment agreements.

The world faces a fundamental need not only for new
international investments, but also for profound
improvements in our national and international policies to
support sustainable development. Achieving a proper balance
between these goals is nothing less than imperative.

David Runnalls   Kathryn S. Fuller
President   President
International Institute for   World Wildlife Fund
Sustainable Development   (WWF–U.S.)

**Private Rights,
Public Problems:
A guide to
NAFTA's
controversial
chapter on
investor rights**

Acknowledgements

This guide was written by Dr. Howard Mann, an Ottawa-based international lawyer specializing in the environmental, trade and investment elements of international sustainable development law. He is an Associate of IISD and a long-time analyst of the sustainable development implications of international investment and trade law.

Aaron Cosbey of IISD served as manager of the project and reviewer of the text, in collaboration with David Schorr of WWF–U.S. Particularly helpful advice and comments came from a panel of peer reviewers that included Steve Shrybman and Monica Araya. The opinions expressed in this guide are those of IISD and WWF, however, and should not be attributed to these individuals. Thanks are also due to Konrad von Moltke, Luke Peterson and Jennifer Castleden of IISD for their comments on the text.

An online version of this guide, as well as details on IISD's Investment Law and Sustainable Development Project of which this book is a part, can be found at http://www.iisd.org/trade/investment. Also see the WWF–U.S. investment site at http://www.worldwildlife.org/commerce.

The guide was jointly produced by IISD and WWF–U.S. as part of an international effort to raise awareness on the full implications of investment law. Its production was made possible through the generous financial support of the Ford Foundation.

**Private Rights,
Public Problems:**
A guide to
NAFTA's
controversial
chapter on
investor rights

1.

Chapter 11 and the concerned citizen

"Chapter 11" is a well-known phrase in the United States: it is the term used when someone seeks court protection to avoid an impending bankruptcy. But under the North American Free Trade Agreement—NAFTA—Chapter 11 has another meaning. It is the part of NAFTA that deals with the protection of foreign investors from Canada, Mexico and the United States when they invest in one of the other NAFTA countries.[1] For some, Chapter 11 is a vital requirement in promoting the free flow of capital in an increasingly open North American market. For others, Chapter 11 represents another kind of bankruptcy—the bankruptcy of public policy and international law-making in the era of economic globalization.

1.1 Two basic concerns

What does Chapter 11 do, and why are so many citizens' groups (as well as government leaders) concerned?

Chapter 11 is designed to protect the interests of foreign investors, and to liberalize international investment. But in recent years, citizens' groups (and some government officials) in all three NAFTA countries have become increasingly concerned that the effects of Chapter 11 might take these goals too far. The major focus of their concern relates to the ability of corporations, notably foreign corporations, to use Chapter 11's provisions in ways that can restrict or even negate governments' ability to protect human welfare and the environment. These concerns can be summed up in two basic claims brought by Chapter 11's critics:

• Chapter 11 can undermine efforts to enact new laws and regulations in the public interest, in particular to protect the environment and human health.

• Chapter 11 can require governments to pay compensation to polluters to stop polluting, even if their activities have an adverse impact on public health and welfare.

1.2 The purpose of this guide

Private Rights, Public Problems evaluates these concerns objectively, and in straightforward, clear language. To do this

Private Rights,
Public Problems:
A guide to
NAFTA's
controversial
chapter on
investor rights

the guide goes back to the beginning, looking first at why international agreements on investment came about, and then at why this trend was extended to NAFTA. The guide then briefly lays out the main components of Chapter 11. It then tries to explain why foreign investment law—an area that has been developing for over 50 years without much public controversy—has suddenly become a flash point for international concern.

The guide then looks in detail at the main components of Chapter 11: what they cover, the obligations they impose and the enforcement tools they provide. From this analysis, it concludes that Chapter 11 does indeed threaten governments' ability to protect the public interest in terms of environmental, human health and other social issues.

Many in civil society have taken the view that trade and investment agreements generally prevent governments from doing what they are elected to do: protect the interests of the people they serve. This guide does not take a general position against investment or trade agreements. On the contrary, it recognizes the important role such agreements must play if trade and investment are to reduce poverty and foster sustainable development around the world. But each such agreement must be evaluated on its own merits to assess its contribution towards these goals. What this book looks at are the concerns that have arisen from the current construction and application of Chapter 11: is it working in a way that produces appropriate and acceptable results? And if not, why not?

This approach allows us to learn from NAFTA's first six years of operation. Having concluded there are serious flaws in the design and operation of Chapter 11, we look to the future: what can be done to fix the problems, and what can be done to ensure the same mistakes are not repeated in other investment negotiations, notably in the Free Trade Area of the Americas (FTAA) negotiations and the World Trade Organization (WTO)?[2] Given the possible creation of new, more extensive, investment agreements, this publication finishes by asking a fundamentally important question: can the flaws in Chapter 11 be repaired with new language, or is there a deeper flaw that goes more broadly to the chapter's foundation?

**Private Rights,
Public Problems:**
A guide to
NAFTA's
controversial
chapter on
investor rights

Endnotes

1 To reference the full text of NAFTA, including Chapter 11, see http://www.nafta-sec-alena.org/english/index.htm.

2 The FTAA process includes 34 countries in the western hemisphere from the Arctic to the Antarctic—all countries but Cuba. The negotiating process is expected to conclude in 2003 or 2005. The World Trade Organization is actively considering whether to include more investment issues in any new round of global trade negotiations.

**Private Rights,
Public Problems:**
A guide to
NAFTA's
controversial
chapter on
investor rights

2.

What are international investment agreements, and why was one included in NAFTA?

2.1 International investment agreements: A brief note

Early international investment agreements had two basic purposes. First, the agreements were intended to protect foreign investors from nefarious or discriminatory acts by the "host country"—the country in which the investment is made. Throughout the early 1950s and into the 1960s and 1970s, a number of foreign investments were either directly taken by host governments without compensation, or were closed down and had their assets stripped in less direct ways. This was at a time of well-defined East-West political blocs, and of decolonization, two factors that often led to divergent economic and social objectives between foreign investors and their host governments. During this period, the investments were primarily in the form of productive facilities or businesses, such as manufacturing, mining, and oil extraction and production. These types of investments are known as foreign direct investment (FDI).

The political and legal instability that became associated with FDI during this period led lawyers and diplomats to develop bilateral investment treaties (BITs) between the investors' home states and the host countries. These BITs sought to reduce investors' risks by requiring that foreign owned companies should be treated as favourably as domestic companies, and in accordance with other types of obligations that are described in section 5 of this book. Most of the BITs also included provisions for the settlement of disputes, first by arbitration between the home and host states, and later by arbitration directly between the foreign investor and the host state. These treaties were seen as important even where national laws were being updated to protect foreign (and often domestic) investors, because they "locked in" the new domestic laws, and hence the investor protection.

As the web of investment agreements grew, a second purpose emerged—this time from the host country perspective.

Private Rights,
Public Problems:
A guide to
NAFTA's
controversial
chapter on
investor rights

Investment agreements are seen to reduce risks for the foreign investor. Because risk is an important factor in business decisions on when and where to invest, countries that had investment agreements—especially developing countries—found them to be a positive element in attracting foreign investors. Of course other factors are also important: the available resources to run the business, the presence of a skilled labour force, access to markets and so on. But, where these elements were present, countries seeking foreign investment came to believe that having investment agreements gave them an edge over those countries that did not.

While these two purposes related to the protection of investors, in the 1980s another sort of purpose emerged for negotiating international investment regimes: investment liberalization. Investment liberalization rules aim at broadening opportunities for FDI in two main ways. First, they seek an end to restrictions that governments sometimes place on the kinds of foreign investments allowed within their borders (e.g., exclusion from particular economic sectors). Second, they generally forbid a category of practices known as "performance requirements" which attach conditions to investment activity (e.g., requiring investors to use local raw materials or to export a certain percentage of their production). The development of these investment liberalization provisions was underpinned by increasingly prominent free-market economic theory in the 1980s—theory that held restrictions and conditions on foreign investment to be economically inefficient because they distorted patterns of business investments. It was argued that, when combined with the lifting of trade barriers, investment liberalization would lead to a higher level of economic efficiency and ultimately be better for the host countries and businesses alike.

By the end of the 1990s, there were over 1800 bilateral investment treaties in place. Dispute resolution processes had moved from voluntary international mechanisms to binding arbitration that could be initiated by a foreign investor. In addition, investment obligations began to appear in trade agreements such as NAFTA.

Clearly, these sorts of provisions go well beyond the initial scope of investor protection. Today, investment agreements normally reflect the combination of investor protection and investment liberalization objectives.

By the end of the 1990s, there were over 1,800 BITs in place. They had evolved from their early beginnings in several ways. Later agreements had incorporated investment liberalization objectives, as well as those for investor protection. As well, dispute resolution processes moved from voluntary international mechanisms to binding arbitration that could be initiated by a foreign investor. In addition, investment obligations began to appear in *trade* agreements such as the Canada-United States Free Trade Agreement, the Agreement

**Private Rights,
Public Problems:**
A guide to
NAFTA's
controversial
chapter on
investor rights

establishing Mercosur, the European Union agreements, the European Energy Charter and, of course, in NAFTA.[3]

2.2 Why an investment chapter was included in NAFTA

The drafting of NAFTA itself was concluded in 1992. It bound Canada, Mexico and the United States when it entered into force on January 1, 1994, creating what was at the time the world's most populous free trade area.

The main precursor to NAFTA was the Canada-United States Free Trade Agreement, concluded in 1988, which contained provisions on investor protection and on investment liberalization. But since both Canada and the United States had similar legal and economic infrastructures, investor protection was not the key issue. Rather, the main U.S. objective—of such importance that it tied inclusion of an investment chapter to the completion of the overall trade agreement—was investment liberalization in Canada. Canada, for its part, wanted to preserve as many of its foreign investment restrictions as it could. At the end of the day, Canada agreed to significantly reduce its barriers to foreign investments, and both Parties agreed to the types of investor protection provisions generally seen in the BITs at that time. However, the Canada-U.S. Agreement did not include a binding dispute settlement mechanism between the foreign investor and the host state.

With this model in hand, the U.S. sought to expand the investment agreement to the trilateral NAFTA. Of greater importance for the U.S. in the NAFTA case, however, was investor protection in Mexico, given that country's shaky record on treatment of foreign investors. The opportunity to increase FDI into Mexico through vigorous investment liberalization provisions remained an important goal as well. Although Mexican domestic law was changing, U.S. investors wanted a broader range of protections and market access that could not be easily reversed by a subsequent administration.

These objectives were largely supported by Canada for its investors as well. On the other hand, Canada hoped the investment chapter would not lead to any further reduction in its foreign investment management regime, in particular in sectors such as culture and natural resource management.

Mexico, for its part, embraced the goal of attracting new foreign investment. Under the Salinas administration, Mexico had been promoting more open markets and an open investment regime. The inclusion of the investment chapter in

Mexico, for its part, embraced the goal of attracting new foreign investment. Under the Salinas administration, Mexico had been promoting more open markets and an open investment regime. The inclusion of the investment chapter in NAFTA, while originally opposed by Mexico, became seen as a way to "advertise" that the country was indeed a new, safe place to do business.

**Private Rights,
Public Problems:**
A guide to
NAFTA's
controversial
chapter on
investor rights

*Ultimately, Chapter
11 came to include
stronger elements
of investor
protection and
liberalization than
found in the
Canada-U.S. Free
Trade Agreement,
or in any existing
bilateral
investment treaty.*

NAFTA, while originally opposed by Mexico, became seen as a way to "advertise" that the country was indeed a new, safe place to do business. Five and six years later, Mexico became the most steadfast supporter of the NAFTA investment regime, having seen an exponential increase in investments from its NAFTA partners, as well as from European and Japanese investors eager to have better access to the North American market through a low-cost location they now considered "safe."

With NAFTA's goal going beyond trade liberalization to promote a more integrated North American-wide market for goods, services and capital, the economic rationale behind investment liberalization played a large role in shaping the final text of Chapter 11. Ultimately, the chapter came to include stronger elements of investor protection and liberalization than found in the Canada-U.S. Free Trade Agreement, or in any existing BIT.

Endnote

3   The treaties establishing the European Union provide even more extensive protections than other regimes, but in a very different and more encompassing institutional and legal setting. On the other hand, the agreement establishing Mercosur—the common market of the southern core countries of Latin America—is significantly more cautious than NAFTA in its investment provisions, as are the provisions of the EU-Mexico Free Trade Agreement on investment.

3.

Chapter 11 in a nutshell

Private Rights,
Public Problems:
A guide to
NAFTA's
controversial
chapter on
investor rights

In this section, three basic components of Chapter 11 are introduced:

- The scope of coverage: what types of investments and investors are covered, and what types of government actions;

- The rights of foreign investors or, conversely, the obligations that states have towards foreign investors; and

- The process for handling disputes between foreign investors and host countries.

As well, Chapter 11's environmental provisions are discussed. The next section lays out six broad concerns with the application of Chapter 11 to date. Sections 5, 6 and 7 then go into greater depth on how these concerns play out in each of the three basic components listed above.

3.1   The scope of Chapter 11

Chapter 11 provides rights to foreign investors and their investments. A foreign investor is defined as any person or company who makes an investment into another NAFTA Party. Investments are broadly defined, and include the traditional FDI, as well as all types of financial investments, shareholding, secured debts and so on.

Investors and investments are protected, of course, from certain types of measures taken by governments. But governments are many-layered and take many different types of actions, so the definition of "measures" becomes important. Under Chapter 11 the definition is broad: a measure includes all laws adopted by national, state or provincial legislatures; regulations that implement these laws; local or municipal laws and bylaws; and policies that affect government interaction with businesses. Chapter 11 also applies to laws and regulations that existed prior to its entry into force, unless these are specifically excluded by being listed in a special annex. All provincial and state laws in force before 1994 have been excluded as well.

3.2   The rights of investors under Chapter 11

Chapter 11 provides a broad set of investor protection and investment liberalization rights to foreign investors, and

Private Rights,
Public Problems:
A guide to
NAFTA's
controversial
chapter on
investor rights

obligations for governments. The full list is set out in Table 1. This list shows the range of issues investment agreements deal with today, such as damages caused during wartime, taking profits out of the host country, nationalities of senior managers and directors, national treatment, and expropriation provisions. Many of these rights have over the years become a standard part of international investment agreements, without provoking any controversy.

Table 1: Chapter 11's Components at a Glance

Scope of coverage	Rights of investors/ Obligations of governments	Dispute Resolution
■ Foreign investors and foreign investments, Art. 1101, 1139	■ National Treatment, Art. 1102	■ Investor-State Dispute Resolution process (Chapter 11, Section B, Articles 1115–1138)
■ All investors for "performance requirements" obligations, Art. 1106	■ Most-favoured nation treatment, Art. 1103	
	■ Minimum international standards of treatment, Art. 1105(1)	■ State-to-State dispute resolution (Chapter 20 of NAFTA)
■ Government measures, Arts. 1101, 201	■ Compensation for acts of war or civil strife, Art. 1105(2)	
■ Reservations and exceptions for pre-existing measures, state/provincial/ municipal measures, Article 1108, Annex I, III of Chapter 11	■ Prohibitions on performance requirements, Art. 1106	
	■ Prohibitions on senior management nationality requirements, Art. 1107	
	■ Right to transfer profits, revenues, dividends, etc. out of host state, Art. 1109	
■ Excluded sectors, Art. 1108, Annex II of Chapter 11	■ Expropriation and compensation provisions, Art. 1110	
■ Partial exclusion for government procurement, Art. 1108(7, 8)	■ Environmental protection provision, Article 1114	
	■ Non-application of general environmental, health exceptions, Art. 2101.	

**Private Rights,
Public Problems:**
A guide to
NAFTA's
controversial
chapter on
investor rights

This guide focuses on the rights and obligations that have become controversial because of their serious potential for reducing the ability of governments to maintain and protect the public good. These rights and obligations, described in greater detail in Section 6 below, are:

* national treatment and most-favoured nation treatment;

* minimum international standards of treatment;

* prohibitions on performance requirements; and

* prohibitions on expropriation.

3.3   The dispute settlement process

Chapter 11 contains two dispute settlement processes. The predominant process is the investor-state process which, as its name suggests, is initiated directly by the foreign investor against the host state. The results of the process are binding on both participants, and there are very limited opportunities to appeal or review a decision. One arbitrator is appointed by each participant, and the third one is either jointly agreed upon or is appointed by a neutral third Party.

The arbitration takes place with limited public access to the written documents produced for the case, and no public access to the actual proceedings unless all participants agree to open them up (something that has not happened to date). The secrecy surrounding the investor-state process has been a major source of civil society criticism.

As of April 2001, there were 17 such cases known to have been initiated. All of them are described in Annex 2 to this guide.

The normal state-to-state dispute settlement process set out in Chapter 20 of NAFTA is also applicable to Chapter 11. While there have been 17 investor-state cases so far, only one state-to-state case has addressed the investment obligations. This case does have a relationship to environmental issues, but in a context in which the actual standards were never questioned or challenged.[4] As a result, this case has little bearing on the issues discussed here.

3.4   Chapter 11's environmental provisions

Chapter 11 makes only three references to environmental issues. One is a relatively minor reference to the right of dispute panels to hear from environmental experts.[5] Less trivial, but still of limited importance to the issues raised in this guide, are certain exceptions applicable to NAFTA's prohibition on performance requirements.[6]

The arbitration takes place with limited public access to the written documents produced for the case, and no public access to the actual proceedings unless all participants agree to open them up (something that has not happened to date). The secrecy surrounding the investor-state process has been a major source of civil society criticism.

Private Rights,
Public Problems:
A guide to
NAFTA's
controversial
chapter on
investor rights

The environmental language in Chapter 11 that has so far drawn the most public attention is contained in Article 1114, which makes some effort to ensure that NAFTA's investment provisions do not encourage a "race to the bottom" by countries seeking to attract investment through lax environmental laws. Article 1114 has two provisions. The first holds that nothing in Chapter 11 prevents a country from adopting or maintaining an environmental measure that is otherwise consistent with the chapter. This is not particularly meaningful when it is unscrambled: it simply means that nothing in the chapter prevents you from doing what the chapter does not prohibit you from doing.

The second paragraph of Article 1114 is an unprecedented international commitment to avoid relaxing environmental laws as a means of competing for foreign investment. However, the paragraph is couched in partly hortatory language—the core commitment is expressed as a "should" rather than a "shall," but if any Party believes the spirit of commitment is being violated it can require other Parties to enter into consultations. Unlike the investor protection provisions of Chapter 11, there is no mechanism under NAFTA for private Parties to seek enforcement of Article 1114,[7] or for governments to engage in binding dispute settlement with regard to it.

Unlike the investor protection provisions of Chapter 11, there is no mechanism under NAFTA for private Parties to seek enforcement of the Chapter's environmental provisions.

Article 2101 of NAFTA covers general exceptions to NAFTA obligations, including exceptions for environmental measures to protect human, plant and animal life and health, and to conserve natural resources. While these exceptions are made applicable to trade in goods and obligations affecting such trade, they are not made applicable to the investment obligations in Chapter 11, despite the more direct and longer-term environmental impacts that investments can have. [8]

Endnotes

4   This is the Mexico-U.S. Cross-Border Trucking Services case, *Arbitral Panel Established Pursuant to Chapter Twenty, In the Matter of Cross-Border Trucking Services* (Secretariat File No. USA-Mex-98-2008-01), Final Report of the Panel, February 6, 2001.

5   Article 1132 includes environmental experts in a non-exhaustive list of types of experts that may be engaged by panels, subject to the agreement of both disputing Parties.

Private Rights, Public Problems:
A guide to
NAFTA's
controversial
chapter on
investor rights

6 Environmental exceptions to Chapter 11's rules against performance requirements come from paras. 1106 (2) and (6) of the performance requirements article itself (Article 1106). These exceptions give latitude in the application of performance requirements. However, much of the language is modelled after clauses in the WTO General Agreement on Tariffs and Trade that have long raised environmental concerns.

7 The relationship, if any, between Article 1114 and the dispute settlement processes in the North American Agreement on Environmental Cooperation (NAAEC)—NAFTA's so-called environmental side agreement—has never been established. More critical to date than the legal texts, however, has been the reluctance of NAFTA governments to allow the North American Commission on Environmental Cooperation (created under NAAEC) to explore the issue.

8 The exception, discussed above in endnote 6, is the partial application of similar exceptions to Chapter 11's limits on performance requirements.

**Private Rights,
Public Problems:**
A guide to
NAFTA's
controversial
chapter on
investor rights

4.

Why have these provisions become such a concern?

Private Rights,
Public Problems:
A guide to
NAFTA's
controversial
chapter on
investor rights

That Chapter 11 has now become a real concern is beyond doubt. The first real concerns over the potential scope and uses of Chapter 11 arose in the fall of 1996 with the initiation of the *Ethyl v. Canada* case. This was the first time a foreign investor had actually initiated an arbitration under Chapter 11. Few people, however, paid much attention at the time, and those who did speak out were dismissed as anti-free trade alarmists.

Then, in July 1998, Canada basically conceded the Ethyl case—it withdrew the disputed regulation, paid Ethyl Corp. US $13 million (about Cdn $20 million) and signed a letter saying there was no proof that MMT was harmful. The very day after this was announced, a second case challenging another environmental law was initiated (the *S.D. Myers v. Canada* case, since won by that company but now under review by Canadian courts). With these two back-to-back events, the concerns became more profound.[9]

Since that time, the list of investor-state cases brought in opposition to environmental policies has rapidly expanded. As of March 2001, there have been 10 cases (out of a total of 17) brought against environmental and natural resource management measures, including cases involving hazardous waste management decisions, maintenance of clean drinking water, and gasoline additives barred in other jurisdictions. Perhaps the best known case so far, because of its high profile challenge to an American environmental measure, is *Methanex v. United States*, in which a Canadian corporation is suing the United States for almost a billion U.S. dollars, claiming that it has lost profits and market value as a result of California's plan to ban a suspected carcinogen that has been leaking from fuel tanks into its drinking water supply.

As of March 2001, there have been 10 cases (out of a total of 17) brought against environmental and natural resource management measures, including cases involving hazardous waste management decisions, maintenance of clean drinking water, and gasoline additives barred in other jurisdictions.

By June of 1999, the three NAFTA environment ministers, meeting collectively as the governing Council to the Commission for Environmental Cooperation, recognized the emerging problems in a statement that reaffirmed the sovereign right of each government to protect the environment.[10] Efforts were then being made, but have since ended, to discuss NAFTA Chapter 11 in the Free Trade Commission, NAFTA's governing body, which comprises of the trade ministers of the three

**Private Rights,
Public Problems:**
A guide to
NAFTA's
controversial
chapter on
investor rights

countries. By the end of the year 2000, trade ministers and trade-focused observers were recognizing the problem as well.[11] And, as this guide was being prepared, press reports indicated that the NAFTA Parties might be preparing to revisit their initial discussions on the matter.[12]

How did six years of experience with Chapter 11 create such widespread recognition of problems, when the critics in its early days were so easily dismissed? The remainder of this section presents six central factors underlying the troubling evolution of Chapter 11.

4.1 From shield to sword

One of the key factors in Chapter 11's rise to infamy is also one of the least tangible. This is the change in use of investor protections from a protective "shield" to a strategic, aggressive "sword."

Threats to use Chapter 11 are now a routine corporate lobbying instrument, and are given added impact by the broad scope tribunals have given the obligations in the initial cases.

Investment agreements have traditionally been thought of as recourses of last resort, aimed at protecting an investor through extraordinary means in extraordinary circumstances. Under Chapter 11, however, these provisions are now being turned into a means to fend off proposed new regulations, lobby for or against specific government actions, and generally to preserve or gain a competitive position. Threats to use Chapter 11 are now a routine lobbying instrument, and are given added impact by the broad scope tribunals have given the obligations in the initial cases. This fundamental shift—from protective shield to strategic weapon—means that the drafters of future investment agreements must carefully consider how the provisions can be used not just to protect an investor, but also as a strategic weapon against a government when investor interests are affected. As the BITs that existed before 1992 were never used in this way, the drafters of Chapter 11 gave no consideration to this type of strategic use.

4.2 Broad interpretation of the obligations

Despite the initial pooh-poohing by the trade community, several of the interpretations of Chapter 11 to date have actually outdone the predictions of civil society doomsayers. A key reason for this appears to be the relationship between Chapter 11 and other parts of NAFTA. The coverage of Chapter 11 can, it now seems, extend to measures covered by other parts of the agreement.

For example, a trade measure that blocks a product coming into Canada and is covered by Chapter 3 on Trade in Goods or by Chapter 9 on Standards-Related Measures can apparently be contested by a foreign investor under Chapter 11 as well.

**Private Rights,
Public Problems:**
A guide to
NAFTA's
controversial
chapter on
investor rights

There seem to be two different routes now by which this can be done. One is to argue that a measure that may be covered by these other chapters is also covered by Chapter 11, from the perspective of the investment rules. A second way, worrying in its breadth, is to argue that when a government breaches other international obligations (such as NAFTA Chapters 3 or 9) it thereby also breaches Chapter 11's obligation to treat investors in accordance with minimum international standards.[13]

Metalclad v. Mexico, and *S.D. Myers v. Canada*, two of the first cases to be decided, provide examples of this type of broad interpretation of Chapter 11's obligations. In these cases provisions on trade-related obligations from other parts of NAFTA were incorporated directly into the obligations of Chapter 11, *even though there is no reference to them in the Chapter 11 provisions*. Governments in these cases were held, for example, to requirements for transparency and for least-trade restrictiveness—key trade law principles, but not principles set out in the Chapter 11 *investment* provisions. This way of viewing Chapter 11 has resulted in the broadest interpretations of an investor-protection regime ever seen, and was not anticipated when Chapter 11 was negotiated. Under this approach, any international trade obligation, and potentially any other international law obligations, which have traditionally been the subject of state-to-state disputes are now also open for disputes between investors and states under Chapter 11.

4.3 Narrow interpretation of the objectives

Courts that are asked to interpret and apply an agreement's obligations will often do so in light of the agreement's stated objectives. These are normally found in the agreement's preamble, or other special references, and can express broad political, economic and social goals. Chapter 11 has no such references specific to itself, and so several Tribunals have read the objectives of the NAFTA as a whole (found in the Preamble and Objectives sections) as the objectives applicable to Chapter 11.

Their reading of those objectives has at times been selective, however. In the *Metalclad* case, the Tribunal stated the three objectives it believed were relevant to interpreting the provisions of Chapter 11:[14]

• To increase transparency in government regulations and activity;

• To substantially increase investment opportunities; and

• To ensure a predictable commercial framework for investors.

**Private Rights,
Public Problems:**
A guide to
NAFTA's
controversial
chapter on
investor rights

*The Metalclad
decision's reading
of Chapter 11's
objectives
ignores the
counterbalances
included in the
preamble of
NAFTA relating to
environmental
protection and
sustainable
development as
equal goals.*

This reading of the objectives for Chapter 11 ignores the counterbalances included in the preamble of NAFTA relating to environmental protection and sustainable development as equal goals (see Box 1). Clearly, identifying only such investor-focused objectives creates a high risk of an imbalanced interpretation of Chapter 11's obligations. In *Metalclad*, for example, the Tribunal went so far as to argue that it was the objective of Chapter 11 to *ensure the successful implementation* of investment initiatives, although this objective is never stated in NAFTA itself. This led to an extremely broad interpretation of the Chapter 11 obligations, as discussed in section 6.2.

BOX 1: NAFTA's Environmental and Sustainability-Related Objectives:

– Undertake each of the preceding (i.e., the economic objectives) in a manner consistent with environmental protection and conservation;

– Preserve their flexibility to safeguard the public welfare;

– Promote sustainable development;

– Strengthen the development and enforcement of environmental laws and regulations; and

– Protect, enhance and enforce basic workers' rights.

From: NAFTA's Preamble, concluding paragraphs

A more balanced approach was seen, at least on the surface, in the *S.D. Myers* decision, which noted the environmental objectives expressed in the preamble to NAFTA. Yet, even with this recognition, the *S.D. Myers* decision went on to incorporate actual trade rules from other parts of NAFTA directly into the interpretation of Chapter 11. It also went on to use NAFTA's trade objectives to help interpret two international environmental agreements relating to the transboundary movement of hazardous waste that were negotiated in a completely unrelated context, leaving them subject to a distorted interpretation.[15]

These cases show how broad objectives related to trade liberalization can impact on the interpretation of investment rules (and even on international environmental agreements).

When the objectives are not balanced, or are invoked in an unbalanced manner, the effect is unbalanced interpretations. This highlights the need to have specific objectives for an investment agreement or an investment chapter in a larger agreement. It also highlights the need to ensure that such objectives are clearly and expressly balanced.

4.4 Rights, but no responsibilities

Chapter 11 focuses exclusively on investor rights, in particular those of foreign investors, and their equivalent government obligations. There are no responsibilities cast upon the investor. And the main dispute resolution process—the investor-state process—can only be initiated by foreign investors against the host government.

Foreign investors are thus granted special international law-based rights and the means to enforce them. Once these rights were turned into a strategic weapon as opposed to a protective instrument, they became available to use to "fight" against new public policy measures that had a negative impact on the corporation. While it is certainly true that Chapter 11 does not exclude a foreign investor from the obligation to follow applicable laws in the host state, it is also true that Chapter 11 has provided these investors with special rights to challenge those very laws, or any proposed laws that might affect their interests. There are no counterbalancing rights of governments or obligations on foreign investors that limit the scope or exercise of the rights. Indeed, this has already been seen in the review of the limited and non-binding nature of Chapter 11's environmental provisions.

The granting of rights without commensurate responsibilities is inherently dangerous. This is no less the case when those rights come from international law.

The granting of rights without commensurate responsibilities is inherently dangerous. This is no less the case when those rights come from international law.

4.5 Lack of political constraints

The traditional state-to-state model of international law arbitrations provides important political checks and balances before an arbitration is initiated. A state thinking about starting a case needs to consider other political relationships, with the state in question or with other states, as well as domestic political issues. How, for example, will starting a case against an environmental law relate to a government's own environmental protection policies, or to its image as "green?" These types of political factors force a government's decision to initiate a case to pass through a "filter" of broader public interest.

**Private Rights,
Public Problems:**
A guide to
NAFTA's
controversial
chapter on
investor rights

Under Chapter 11, investors have only their self-interest to consider. To some extent, this may have political dimensions, for example concerning their relationships with officials in the host state. Many companies, however, are quite comfortable operating in a context of legal "battle" with governments in the pursuit of their corporate interest. Indeed, trade law experts and negotiators have expressed the view that private participants in the trade law system are not constrained by anything other than their self-interest, which strongly differentiates them from governments that have to balance many public policy objectives in making any decision.[16] This situation is even more likely to exist when the investor is from a foreign country and might be seeking to enter a market or preserve market share that is jeopardized by a government action. Foreign investors are often likely to consider in very stark terms the question: "So what is there to lose by trying this?"

4.6 Lack of public access and accountability

Section 7 will discuss Chapter 11's arbitration process. The lack of transparency and public access in that process has drawn heavy criticism from a number of quarters. In addition, Chapter 11 must be understood as being embedded in a broader NAFTA regime that is itself remarkably short of the kinds of transparent and accessible checks and balances that are common for most bodies having significant impacts on governments.

The key NAFTA institution is the Free Trade Commission, composed of the trade ministers of the three NAFTA countries. This Commission generally meets just once a year, and must rely to a large extent on the staff that prepares its meetings. While the agreement provides for the creation of a NAFTA Secretariat, it also indicates this is to be composed of three national sections located in each capital city.[17] A subsequent informal agreement among the three Parties did call for the establishment of a NAFTA Secretariat in Mexico City, but this never happened. As a result of this and other closed internal processes, it is very difficult to obtain an overview of continuing developments within NAFTA. Also, the NAFTA Secretariat has no responsibility for managing or documenting the dispute settlement process. This has created a certain opaqueness to NAFTA that is taken to a deeper level, as will be seen below, in the Chapter 11 dispute settlement process itself.

Private Rights,
Public Problems:
A guide to
NAFTA's
controversial
chapter on
investor rights

Endnotes

9 Ultimately, these Chapter 11 cases also became important in a broader international context, providing concrete evidence of what investment agreements could do as a rallying point for the non-governmental community to oppose the OECD's negotiations on a Multilateral Investment Agreement. The protests were a major factor in the collapse of those negotiations.

10 The statement is found in the Final Communique, Commission for Environmental Cooperation, Annual Council Meeting, Banff, Alberta, June 28, 1999.

11 Edward Graham, *Fighting the Wrong Enemy: Antiglobal Activists and Multinational Enterprises* (Washington D.C.: Institute for International Economics, 2000); Gary Hufbauer *et al.*, *NAFTA and the Environment: Seven years Later* (Washington D.C.: Institute for International Economics, 2000). The scope of the legitimate concerns is not agreed upon by all observers, but the need to carefully review the issues is accepted.

12 See, for example, "Pettigrew Sees Mexican Openness to Clarify NAFTA Investment," *Inside U.S. Trade*, 2 March 2001, 13–14.

13 This argument has been used in at least two Chapter 11 cases: *S.D. Myers v. Canada* and the first case, *Ethyl v. Canada*. This is also seen in Article 1112 of NAFTA.

14 See paras. 70–75 of the decision on how the objectives were set out and applied.

15 These are the *Basel Convention of the Control of Transboundary Movements of Hazardous Wastes and Their Disposal*, completed in 1989 under UN auspices, and the bilateral *Agreement Between the Government of Canada and the Government of the United States of America Concerning the Transboundary Movement of Hazardous Wastes*, originally completed in 1986 and amended in 1992.

16 Jonathan Fried, "Globalization and International Law—Some Thoughts for Citizens and States," *Queen's Law Journal*, 23, (1997), 251.

17 NAFTA, Article 2002.

**Private Rights,
Public Problems:**
A guide to
NAFTA's
controversial
chapter on
investor rights

5.

What does Chapter 11 cover?

Private Rights,
Public Problems:
A guide to
NAFTA's
controversial
chapter on
investor rights

5.1 The broad approach to defining "investors" and "investments"

Chapter 11 covers foreign investors and their investments, providing similar protections to each. Foreign investors are those from one NAFTA Party that invests into the territory of another NAFTA Party. Because an "investor" is defined merely as anyone who makes an investment, it is the definition of investment that is really critical.

"Investment" is very broadly defined in Article 1139 of NAFTA. It includes a business ("enterprise"); shares in a business; a debt security in a business in some cases; a loan to a business; interests entitling the holder to a share of profits; income or the proceeds of a dissolution of a business; real estate bought for business purposes; and a very broad concept of "interests" arising from the commitment of financial or human resources to economic activity. This definition includes direct investments in a business facility such as a factory or retail store or distribution center, as well as portfolio investments such as stocks or bonds.

There is, in fact, very little limit to the scope of what Chapter 11 defines as a protectable investment. In an important case, *S.D. Myers v. Canada*, the Tribunal ruled the scope of "investment" includes such assets as market share in a sector, and access to markets in the host state, whether or not the investor even owns a physical plant or retail store in that country.[18] In short, almost any kind of business *activity* can constitute an investment that is subject to protection.

The unintended effect of this approach is to blur the distinction between investment and trade, offering Chapter 11 protections to companies that only seek to sell goods or services without committing any capital investment to the foreign country. As already noted, this is a much broader scope than is found historically in international investment law, which protected the property and operations of foreign direct investments.

Foreign investments are covered at all stages of their lifecycle, from the initial effort to make the investment through to the final disposition of assets on its dissolution. Investments made prior to the entry into force of NAFTA are also covered.

There is very little limit to the scope of what Chapter 11 defines as a protectable investment. In S.D. Myers v. Canada, the Tribunal ruled the scope of "investment" includes such assets as market share in a sector, and access to markets in the host state, whether or not the investor even owns a physical plant or retail store in that country.

**Private Rights,
Public Problems:**
A guide to
NAFTA's
controversial
chapter on
investor rights

In general only foreign, not domestic, investors and their investments are covered. The one exception is in Article 1106, which prohibits governments from imposing performance requirements. This prohibition actually applies to *all* investments made in each country, whether by foreign or domestic investors. Unlike foreign investors, however, domestic investors have no recourse to the investor-state process. In fact, it is not yet clear whether there are any legal avenues for domestic investors to enforce this provision.

5.2 Government "measures": a broad and retroactive definition

Chapter 11 applies to any "measure" taken by a national, state, provincial or local government in Canada, Mexico and the United States. "Measure" is not defined in Chapter 11, but is defined in Chapter 2 of NAFTA as including "any law, regulation, procedure, requirement or practice." This list includes policies that may be implemented by a government in the territory of a NAFTA Party. It also includes the procedures leading to the adoption of a law or regulation, and the administrative process leading to a permit, siting, zoning or other type of government decision, and the conduct and results of court cases in domestic courts. In essence any new governmental act, at any level of government, that impacts on an investor may fall within what is covered.

But Chapter 11 also covers existing measures adopted prior to NAFTA coming into effect January 1, 1994, unless they are specifically excluded by being listed in an Annex to NAFTA. Local government, state and provincial measures adopted before 1994 are all exempted.

Chapter 11 applies to all sectors of business activity unless, again, the Parties have excluded them by listing them in an Annex. However, at least some of the provisions of NAFTA will apply to *any* investment. The prohibition on expropriation without compensation, for example, applies to all sectors after an investment is made, even if the sector is listed in an Annex.

Endnote

18 *S.D. Myers v. Canada*, para. 232, stating that Myers' market share in Canada constituted an investment. Also see *Pope & Talbot v. Canada*, para. 96, defining access to U.S. markets by a foreign investment as a protected property interest.

6.

What are the obligations in Chapter 11?[19]

It should be noted at the outset that many of the rights and obligations in Chapter 11 have existed without controversy in international investment agreements for years, even decades. (See Table 1 for a list of the rights and obligations.) Most sound basically reasonable, including the requirement to accord similar treatment to foreign-owned and domestically-owned businesses (national treatment), or to meet minimum international standards for treatment. Thus, it is natural that many people assume benefits can and will flow from such investment agreements.[20] But the question considered in this guide is whether NAFTA's Chapter 11—and especially certain provisions of it as currently crafted and applied—is also producing unsatisfactory, or even unacceptable, outcomes, and if so, why? The discussion in this section will focus on those provisions that are the most relevant to this question, because of their impact on the role of government in maintaining and protecting the public good.

As noted in section 3, Chapter 11 contains several obligations, referred to by trade lawyers as "disciplines," on governments. Four of these will be examined here:

• National treatment and most-favoured nation treatment, Articles 1102–1103;

• Minimum international standards of treatment, Article 1105(1);

• Performance requirement prohibitions, Article 1106; and

• Prohibition of expropriation, Article 1110.

It should be noted that these Chapter 11 rights are independent of each other. In other words, to breach Chapter 11 a government need only violate one of its obligations. Each of the four will be considered below, based on the written text and on the cases that have applied them. A description of each of these cases can be found in Annex 2. All of the decisions discussed, and many of the other case documents are now available on the Internet.[21]

This discussion focuses on legal interpretations of the cases and the longer-term consequences these interpretations

**Private Rights,
Public Problems:**
A guide to
NAFTA's
controversial
chapter on
investor rights

suggest. While each arbitration is tightly tied to its facts, the Tribunal's appreciation of the facts in each case is not subject to public scrutiny as the full record of the cases are not open to the public. (More on this in section 7.) Consequently, the public is really left to consider only the longer-term implications of the Tribunals' legal reasoning.

The Chapter 11 cases initiated to date address issues of fundamental public importance,[22] such as prospective legislation on pharmaceuticals; environmental laws and regulations; the impartiality of the U.S. court system; implementing international agreements (on softwood lumber and hazardous waste); and managing and regulating municipal services and waste disposal. The focus of our discussion is the issues most closely related to the public welfare protection role of governments. Perhaps coincidentally, the cases most closely related to this concern are also the only ones to have been ruled upon by the Arbitral Tribunals to date.

6.1 National treatment, most-favoured nation treatment

A key objective of any investment agreement is to avoid discrimination against investors based on their country of origin. Under Chapter 11, a host government must treat foreign investors and their investments "no less favourably" than it treats domestic investors or investors from other countries. This does not always mean identical treatment, but it does mean that any differences cannot disadvantage the foreign investor relative to domestic or foreign competitors. This is the essence of national treatment and most-favoured nation (MFN) treatment, arguably the most fundamental principles of any trade or investment agreement.

The key to determining how these principles will work in any agreement is the meaning of the term "in like circumstances," since it is when companies are "in like circumstances" that no less favourable treatment must be granted. As a simple example, is an investor seeking to open a factory next to a protected wilderness area in like circumstances to a city-based investor in the same sector? A range of trade law cases give us the understanding that "like circumstances" does not mean the exact same circumstances, but rather *similar* ones. So what criteria or factors should count when one has to decide if two or more different investors are "in like circumstances?" Until the Chapter 11 cases, this issue does not appear to have been addressed in any detail. There was really no understanding on such criteria or factors in the investment context.

**Private Rights,
Public Problems:**
A guide to
NAFTA's
controversial
chapter on
investor rights

The *S.D. Myers* decision now raises a serious concern on this point. One would have thought that comparing like circumstances would involve comparing similar operations located in the host country. S.D. Myers Canada, the investment in this case, operated as a waste broker service—a middleman that exported waste generated in Canada to its parent company's U.S.-based waste disposal operations. The Tribunal, however, went beyond comparing the investment located in Canada with other Canadian-based waste broker services, and asked whether the investor's U.S.-based waste disposal operations were receiving less favourable treatment than that accorded to similar Canadian waste-disposal operations. In the final event the national treatment obligation was applied to the full intended business line of the investor, in its home country as well as in the host country, not just to the investment located within the host country.[23] This represents a remarkable extension of the anticipated scope of the national treatment requirement.

Other kinds of issues are likely to arise in an environmental context. For example, environmental regulation today often includes setting maximum levels of pollution in local air and watersheds. These levels usually mean that newer investors face higher environmental standards than previous investors—they may even be denied permission to operate— since they would represent additional sources of pollution. If a prospective new investor were foreign, would this constitute less favourable treatment than accorded to existing domestic investors? Another question concerns setting limits on transboundary environmental impacts. For example, could Canada or one of its provinces ban the import of electricity from a facility whose pollution spills over into Canada, even if its own electricity producers are allowed to emit similar total amounts of pollution? Would that violate the national treatment requirement for an American company seeking to establish a market share in electricity?

The *S.D. Myers* case does indicate that there could be like circumstances that would nonetheless justify different regulatory treatment in order to protect the public.[24] However, the Tribunal did not go on to apply this statement or provide any more guidance on how it should be applied.

In the end, because of its broad ruling on national treatment and "in like circumstances," the *S.D. Myers* case creates worrying uncertainty as to the latitude companies now have to challenge a measure for violating the national treatment obligation. This worry is compounded by Chapter 11's broad definition of what constitutes an investment, discussed above.

Environmental regulation often includes setting maximum levels of pollution in local air and watersheds. These levels usually mean that newer investors face higher environmental standards than previous investors, since they would represent additional sources of pollution. If a prospective new investor were foreign, would this constitute less favourable treatment than accorded to existing domestic investors?

**Private Rights,
Public Problems:**
A guide to
NAFTA's
controversial
chapter on
investor rights

6.2   Minimum international standards

Like most bilateral investment agreements, Chapter 11
contains provisions requiring host countries to treat foreign
investors in a way that meets minimum international
standards. This requirement is expressed in very general
language as "treatment in accordance with international law,
including fair and equitable treatment and full protection and
security." Exactly what this means has never been
comprehensively spelled out in NAFTA, or in other investment
agreements. Still, when investment provisions were used only
as a shield this created little controversy; it was understood
that the intention was to provide a floor of minimum
standards of fair treatment, regardless of whether domestic
firms were being treated equally badly. But with the change in
the use of the provisions from shield into sword, the lack of
precision simply invites new scope for claims under this
discipline, often coming from different areas of law.

Chapter 11's *Metalclad* decision demonstrates the increasing
significance of this obligation to public welfare law making. In
this case, Mexico was found to violate the minimum
international standards requirements because:[25]

- One level of government (municipal) had failed to live up
  to assurances the tribunal ruled had been made by another
  level (federal), that the waste disposal facility in question
  would be able to operate. The Tribunal ruled that under
  Chapter 11, investors have a right to rely upon such
  assurances (although none of the three NAFTA
  constitutional systems allow federal officials to determine
  the application of the regulations of other levels of
  government);

- Mexico failed to clarify understandings of Mexican law
  upon which the investor relied; the Tribunal ruled the
  government has an obligation to do this if any uncertainty
  arises for the investor;

- Mexico failed to establish clear ways for investors to easily
  know the rules on permits, in breach of the transparency
  obligation in other parts of NAFTA;

- The arbitral Tribunal ruled that a breach of Mexican law
  by a government agency (at any level), as established by the
  Tribunal (not the domestic courts), amounted to a breach
  of minimum international standards, leaving open the
  question of whether this could cover any breach, even if in
  good faith; and because

- *Metalclad* was not notified of a town meeting concerning
  its permit.

The Tribunal summed up its findings by saying that Mexico failed to provide a transparent, predictable framework for business planning and investment, and demonstrated a lack of orderly process and timely disposition in relation to an investor.

This extremely broad reading of minimum international standards requirements was groundbreaking in international investment law. As discussed in section 4.2, it depended in significant part on transparency provisions from other parts of NAFTA that are not mentioned in Chapter 11. This approach of incorporating provisions from outside Chapter 11 was also supported, at least to some extent, in the *S.D. Myers* case.[26] A third case, *Pope and Talbot v. Canada*, was still considering the scope of this obligation at the time of preparing this book, although it had dismissed the company's claims on two other grounds.

The initial assessments of the minimum standards obligation in the Chapter 11 suggested it was not an area of major concern from a broader public welfare perspective.[27] But the *Metalclad* and *S.D. Myers* decisions, along with the obvious uncertainty the Tribunal itself has experienced in the *Pope & Talbot* case, calls those conclusions into question. Can it really be, for example, that governments have an obligation to correct poor legal advice received by an investor? Does one bureaucrat's representation that a certain event will or will not take place under the law of another level of government bind the country at all levels of government? Can a federal government official in this way effectively usurp the decision-making functions of other levels of government? These possibilities suggest standards never before made applicable in domestic law or international law, but they appear to be perilously close to the result in *Metalclad*. Governments will need greater clarity on the meaning of this provision if they are to have any certainty as to their obligations when acting to protect the public good.

6.3 Performance requirements

Prohibitions on performance requirements aim to prevent a host government from imposing conditions on an investor that may limit its ability to achieve economic efficiency and profits. They are, thus, tied to the investment liberalization objectives of the Chapter. Article 1106 prohibits host governments from imposing such requirements as:

* Exporting a given portion of production;

* Using a given level of local inputs or services in business operations, or otherwise showing a preference for domestic goods or services;

**Private Rights,
Public Problems:**
A guide to
NAFTA's
controversial
chapter on
investor rights

- Generating foreign exchange flows based on the firm's levels of imports or exports;

- Using or transferring certain technologies (with some exceptions); or

- Employing specified types or levels of personnel.

It was originally anticipated that this provision would apply only to measures specifically targeted at a foreign investor or its investment. Therefore, even though the provision covered all stages of the investment cycle—from initiating to operating to terminating the investment—it was thought that only a narrow range of measures would be captured. The early cases have shown otherwise. It is now clear that under Chapter 11 even non-discriminatory measures of general application (that is, measures not targeted at a specific investor or sector), both new and pre-existing, can be considered to be performance requirements.[28]

Using this reasoning, it can and has been argued that an import ban on a product used by manufacturers is in effect a requirement to use local substitute products. The result is that foreign investors that might be affected by such a ban are able to bypass the traditional state-to-state process for challenging such trade measures—a process that has been the hallmark of the development of trade law in NAFTA and the WTO—and themselves directly challenge the measure. The expanded use of this provision is worrisome; it may seriously weaken the ability of governments to protect human health and the environment from undesirable imports or exports.

*The "performance
requirements"
article remains a
"sleeper" in the
Chapter 11
arsenal, but one
that has significant
potential.*

No investor has yet won a Chapter 11 claim based on this obligation, though this was a major plank in the *Ethyl* case that Canada settled by withdrawing the measure in question and paying compensation. It remains a "sleeper" in the Chapter 11 arsenal, but one that has significant potential.

6.4 Expropriation

The Chapter 11 provisions on expropriation have been the most debated issue concerning the relation of investor protections to environmental and human welfare protection. Article 1110 of NAFTA requires that any expropriation of a foreign investor's investment be for a public policy purpose *and* be accompanied by compensation. This is consistent with most OECD country approaches to government expropriation, where it is not sufficient for a government to expropriate property simply for a public purpose: it must still provide compensation. The critical question that triggers the provision is what government acts constitute an expropriation, or a

Private Rights,
Public Problems:
A guide to
NAFTA's
controversial
chapter on
investor rights

"taking" in U.S. legal language, of property by a government in the first place, and therefore creates the need for compensation?[29]

The public welfare issues raised here are profound, and difficult. To what extent would Article 1110 be applied to laws and regulations that protect the environment and/or human health from hazardous products, from pollution and from dangerous activities? Can setting high environmental standards amount to expropriation if it impacts on business activities?

Can setting high environmental standards amount to expropriation if it impacts on business activities?

How this fundamental concept of an expropriation should be treated receives little guidance even from the text of the Chapter 11 itself. Article 1110 prohibits three types of expropriation—direct expropriation, indirect expropriation, and measures tantamount to expropriation. The cases to date have held that these last two terms have the same meaning: measures that do not directly take investment property, but which amount to the same thing. A high enough business tax levied on a specific firm, for example, would eventually have the same effect as direct expropriation.

One critical issue that has come into focus is the way Article 1110 relates to what is called the exercise of "police powers" by a country enacting a measure.[30] Under the traditional international law concept of the exercise of police powers, when a state acted in a non-discriminatory manner to protect public goods such as its environment, the health of its people or other public welfare interests, such actions were understood to fall outside the scope of what was meant by expropriation. Such acts were simply not covered by the concept of expropriation, were not a taking of property, and no compensation was payable as a matter of international law. Stated simply, if the police powers rule is recognized under the expropriation provision in Chapter 11, then environmental and human health protection laws or regulations will not be considered expropriations so long as they are non-discriminatory and not so unlike the normal exercise of police powers in a given jurisdiction so as to be considered confiscatory.[31] If the rule is not recognized, on the other hand, then even normal exercises of a government's regulatory authority may be considered expropriations requiring payment of compensation.

The scope of a state's legitimate police powers is, of course, not always simple to determine, and may depend on the type of law or regulation in question. For example, protective measures that limit polluting emissions, establish controls or bans on certain hazardous products, would generally be

**Private Rights,
Public Problems:**
A guide to
NAFTA's
controversial
chapter on
investor rights

considered routine exercises of police power. Measures that take land to create a national park, on the other hand, are generally compensated for in most legal systems and may well not be excluded by the police powers rule. Still, the question of what constitutes a normal (or non-confiscatory) exercise of police powers varies in some measure in accordance with national custom and practice.

One of the most disturbing aspects of NAFTA, however, is the current tendency of Chapter 11 tribunals to ignore traditional approaches to expropriation law in a manner that ultimately threatens to severely narrow or even extinguish the doctrine of legitimate police powers. The most direct of these cases is the *Metalclad* decision. Rather than undertake an analysis of whether the Mexican government acted in a manner inconsistent with a normal (non-confiscatory) exercise of its police powers, the Tribunal says expressly and concisely that "The Tribunal need not decide or consider the motivation or intent of the adoption" of the environmental measure in question in that case.[32] Instead, the test that was used in *Metalclad* considered only the scale of impact of a challenged measure on an investment, and whether there was a significant impact on "the use or reasonably-to-be-expected economic benefit of property, even if not to the obvious benefit of the host State."[33] This same approach is repeated in the *Pope & Talbot v. Canada* decision.[34] Neither of these cases, however, provides any real detail on what constitutes a significant impact.[35]

Following this reasoning, regardless of the purpose, compensation must be paid if there is a significant impact. This is alarming since any environmental law worth adopting will affect business operations, and therefore will have a significant impact on the business in question.

While a Chapter 11 tribunal in one other case, the *S.D. Myers* case, did say that government regulatory action is not normally understood as being expropriation, the impact of the case remains unclear. Unfortunately, the decision creates a genuine ambiguity; it states that the main reason the measure in that case does not amount to an expropriation is that it is a temporary one with a temporary impact. [36] One implication is that if the measure had been permanent, it would have been considered confiscatory even though it was the kind of government action usually considered a legitimate exercise of police power.

The most critical point of these initial cases is that they turn to the scale of impact as the critical test of whether a governmental action amounts to expropriation. This approach not only limits the scope of the police powers rule, but also would effectively eliminate this traditional international law test from consideration in the review of an expropriation claim. Following this reasoning, regardless of the purpose, compensation must be paid if there is a significant impact. This is alarming since *any environmental*

**Private Rights,
Public Problems:**
A guide to
NAFTA's
controversial
chapter on
investor rights

law worth adopting will affect business operations and may
often end the use of, or trade in, certain products, and
therefore will have a significant impact on the business in
question. This would reverse a well-accepted tenet of sound
environmental policy: that polluters should bear the cost of
their pollution, rather than enjoy a right to be paid not to
pollute.

The expropriation provision of Chapter 11 has accordingly
given rise to the most heated criticism from civil society, and
the experience of the first few cases seems to have justified their
concerns. No matter how needed or valuable a new piece of law
or regulation, the odds against it will steadily stack up as
regulators tally the costs of potential compensation claims from
affected businesses under Chapter 11's expropriation
provisions. Indeed, if governments have to guess whether a
measure to protect the environment or human health is
covered by the concept of expropriation, it could have (and
already appears to be having) a significant impact on the
freedom of governments to enact strong regulations to protect
the environment or other aspects of the public welfare.

6.5   Summary: The impact of the Chapter 11 obligations

The key point to be drawn from the analysis presented here is
that the current interpretations of NAFTA's Chapter 11 can
have a significant and determinative negative impact on
governmental decision-making in relation to the public
interest. In fact they already have. In Canada, for example,
only two new environmental laws have been adopted at the
federal level since NAFTA came into force, and both have
been challenged under Chapter 11.[37] One was repealed as a
result, with $13M in compensation paid. The other was ruled
a breach of Chapter 11 and a damages award is pending.

This critical impact arises from the interpretations that have
now required governments to compensate investors for any
costs or losses they incur as a result of the adopting new laws.
In the environmental context, this has already begun to turn
the polluter pays principle into a "pay the polluter" principle.
Whatever the merits of any given case, the combined impact
is deeply worrying: it raises serious doubts whether any
NAFTA national or sub-national government can regulate to
protect the environment without a significant risk of having
to pay compensation to private corporations. Indeed, it is
unclear under whether there is any safe harbor for
environmental, human health and other new regulations that
have an impact on foreign investors under the current
interpretations of NAFTA's Chapter 11.

*In Canada, only
two new
environmental
laws have been
adopted at the
federal level since
NAFTA came into
force, and both
have been
successfully
challenged under
Chapter 11.*

While they cannot say so publicly, fewer and fewer environmental regulators are prepared to take the risks now associated with the legal uncertainties and huge claims for compensation under Chapter 11.

The result of these developments is that many regulatory agencies in government become increasingly reluctant to act. This phenomenon is known as "regulatory chill." While they cannot say so publicly, fewer and fewer environmental regulators are prepared to take the risks now associated with the legal uncertainties and huge claims for compensation under Chapter 11. However unintended this result may or may not have been, it is an apparent and important result.

The existing decisions are arguably incorrect in their interpretation of the language and intent behind the Chapter 11 provisions, and they may be subject to correction by later tribunals. This, however, is only a possibility, and for the moment the current interpretations are all that investors, government and others have to work with.

Solutions to the problems identified here, as well as to those found in the next section on the investor-state process, are considered in section 8.

Endnotes

19 Significant portions of what follows are derived from Howard Mann & Monica Araya, *An Investment Regime for the Americas: Challenges and Opportunities for Sustainability* (New Haven, CT, USA: Yale Center for Environmental Law and Policy, 2001); and Howard Mann, "International Environment Law, Chapter 11," *Year in Review Issue, 2000, The International Lawyer*, Vol. 35, Summer, 2001, forthcoming.

20 It is difficult to actually quantify the benefits investment agreements provide to host countries. While they are presumed to play a role in attracting foreign investment—or at least the absence today of such an agreement is presumed to be a negative factor against investments—the precise evidence remains unclear to date.

21 In the absence of a comprehensive Chapter 11 web site hosted by the NAFTA Secretariat or any NAFTA government, the most up-to-date-source is a private web page found at http://www.naftalaw.org. See the introduction to Annex 2 for other government and non-government web sites with relevant documents.

22 This has now been recognized directly by at least one Chapter 11 case: *Methanex v. United States*. See Decision of the Tribunal on Petitions from Third Parties to Intervene as "Amici Curiae," para. 49. Available at http://www.iisd.org/pdf/methanex_tribunal _first_amicus_decision.pdf.

23 These issues are discussed at pages 52–59 of the *S.D. Myers* decision.

24 *S.D. Myers v. Canada*, para. 250.

25 See paras. 75–100 of the *Metalclad* decision.

26 See paras. 258–269 of the *S.D. Myers* decision.

27 E.g. Howard Mann and Konrad von Moltke, "NAFTA's Chapter 11 and the Environment: Addressing the Impacts of the Investor-State Process on the Environment." IISD Working Paper. (Winnipeg: IISD, 1999.)

28 *S.D. Myers v. Canada,* paras. 289–300; *Pope & Talbot v. Canada,* paras. 74; and in the *Ethyl Corp. v. Canada,* Decision on Jurisdiction, paras. 62–64. There is no jurisprudence to the contrary.

29 The key issue of what constitutes a "taking" is widely debated in the United States in particular, where the full scope of a constitutional protection of private property rights remains unresolved. Most countries give public authorities wide latitude before recognizing a "taking." In the United States, however, this issue has continued to be widely debated, and has a primary constitutional law dimension. One of the factors that has made Chapter 11 particularly disconcerting to U.S. environmentalists, and now increasingly environmentalists and other observers in all three NAFTA Parties, is the growing prospect that a fundamental question of constitutional law in the U.S. and one of enormous practical implications for all environmental regulators—may now be decided not through the development of domestic case law but through the essentially unappealable rulings of *ad hoc* Chapter 11 tribunals meeting behind closed doors in a process modeled after private arbitration and based on non-domestic sources of law.

30 This issue was first raised and explored in Mann and von Moltke, 1999, op. cit., supra at 27.

31 Measures within the normal scope of police powers rule would still be subject to review under the provisions of Chapter 11 on national treatment and minimum international standards, among others.

32 *Metalclad,* para. 111. The measure in question was the creation of an ecological reserve that included the land owned by *Metalclad,* thereby ending its possible use for siting a hazardous waste management facility, as *Metalclad* intended. Had the Tribunal held that such a change of land use, while in the public interest, still requires compensation to be paid to the landowners, as is the case in almost all OECD and many other countries, one would have at least found some analysis of the issues relevant to the application of the police powers rule.

33 *Metalclad,* para. 103.

34 *Pope & Talbot,* paras. 96–105

35 To constitute an expropriation, it can be argued that traditional international legal analysis has required that an investor lose all or essentially all of the value of an investment through a government action that is so far beyond the normal exercise of police powers as to be confiscatory in nature. In the United States, the "loss of all value" doctrine and the question of normal police powers have been related, because the "value" of a property

**Private Rights,
Public Problems:**
A guide to
NAFTA's
controversial
chapter on
investor rights

has been considered as subject to the routine exercise of local regulatory power. Thus, an investor has usually been held to enjoy a reasonable expectation to profit from his or her property only to the extent possible under legitimate applications of the police power. The full analysis of these types of issues under national and international law is complex and beyond the scope of this guide.

36 *S.D. Myers v. Canada*, paras. 279–287.

37 A "new law" here means one addressing a new substance or situation not previously regulated. Updates to previously existing laws have not been challenged to date.

7.

Enforcing the foreign investor's rights: The investor-state arbitration process and its democratic deficits

This section looks at the investor-state process, with a particular focus on its absence of democratic safeguards. When looking at the Chapter 11 experience, it is important to remember the high degree of public importance that can be attached to Chapter 11 cases. Where international arbitration was originally conceived as addressing private matters between businesses or between business and a government, this is not the case with Chapter 11 to date, in which important questions of public interest are increasingly being litigated.

7.1   What is the investor-state process and how is it started?

Simply stated, the investor-state process is an international arbitration process between a foreign investor and the host government. A chart of the process is presented in Box 2. The process is started by a foreign investor that invokes its right under Chapter 11 to do so. The first step is to issue what is called a notice of intent to submit a claim to arbitration. This is followed by a consultation and cooling down period of at least 90 days before the actual arbitration can be started by the claimant sending a "notice of arbitration" to the NAFTA Party involved.

When sending the notice of arbitration, the investor chooses one of three internationally recognized arbitration processes operating under the United Nations Commission on International Trade Law (UNCITRAL) or the International Centre for the Settlement of Investment Disputes (ICSID), both of which have been operating for many years.[38]

The notice of intent and notice of arbitration are always sent to the national government of the NAFTA Party, even if the disputed measure is from a state, provincial or local government. It is the national government that is responsible to conduct the arbitration itself and can ultimately be liable

Private Rights,
Public Problems:
A guide to
NAFTA's
controversial
chapter on
investor rights

for any awards against the country, even if the actions that give rise to an award are actions of a state or province.

7.2 Appointment of the arbitral Tribunal

The Tribunal is a three-person body that hears evidence and makes rulings in the cases. Once the notice of arbitration is sent, the investor and state then each nominate their own arbitrator to the Tribunal. A third, neutral arbitrator is either agreed on by the Parties or is appointed by the Secretary General of ICSID from the ICSID Panel of Arbitrators.

Box 2: Sample Flowchart of Investor-State Dispute Settlement Process

- Notice of intent
- Minimum 90-day period of consultations
- Notice of arbitration
- Appointment of arbitral tribunal
- Statement of claim (often accompanies Notice of Arbitration)
- Statement of defence
- Opportunity for friends of the court "*amicus*" petition
- Reply to statement of defence
- Rejoinder to reply
- Opportunity for friends of the court "*amicus*" petition
- Filing of evidence, witness statements
- Cross-examinations
- Filing of full written arguments (Memorial of claimant, Memorial of defendant Party, Reply, Rejoinder)
- Oral hearings[i]
- Possible subsequent written briefs
- Decision
- Possible claim for judicial review/appeal
- Payment of award

**Private Rights,
Public Problems:**
A guide to
NAFTA's
controversial
chapter on
investor rights

The ability of each side to choose "its" arbitrator is an important difference between regular courts and arbitrations, especially when it relates to challenges to public policy issues, and is one of the most controversial elements of the investor-state process. This approach makes sense when only issues of private law—such as compliance with a contract, or responsibility for damage to a shipment—are at stake. It is problematic when issues of public welfare and public policy are placed against private interests.

With limited exceptions, the arbitrators appointed to date have had primarily commercial law backgrounds and experience. This does not, of course, mean that the arbitrators are unaware of public policy issues or are in any way unprofessional. However, this factor can work to reduce the opportunities for diverse understandings of, and approaches to, the issues raised. The discussion so far in this guide makes it clear that the Tribunals face important issues of public welfare, in the end trying to find a balance between investor rights and other public policy objectives like environmental protection.

The ability of each side to choose "its" arbitrator is problematic when issues of public welfare and public policy are placed against private interests.

Once the Tribunal is chosen, it operates under the rules of procedure of the ICSID or UNCITRAL process chosen by the investor. In all three cases, the rules are fairly similar, allowing for the filing of legal arguments, presentation of evidence, cross-examination of witnesses, oral arguments, and finally the decision of the Tribunal. The rules in each process give the Tribunal a significant amount of ability to manage its own proceedings to fit the needs of the case at hand.

7.3 Are there any constraints on initiating a case?

As described earlier, private investors face no political constraints when deciding whether to initiate an investor-state case. The only real constraint is the need to carefully follow the procedural steps set out in Section B of Chapter 11. Most of these provisions are rather mundane procedural steps, such as ensuring six months have gone by since the measure was taken, acting within three years of the measure being taken, ensuring a 90-day consultation period after the notice of intent to arbitrate is submitted, and so on.

The most important of these procedural steps is for the investor to waive all domestic litigation rights for damages arising from the contested government measure. Other actions can still be run in parallel to a Chapter 11 case, such as injunctions, declaratory relief (such as a declaration that a measure is unconstitutional), or extraordinary relief (such as

**Private Rights,
Public Problems:**
A guide to
NAFTA's
controversial
chapter on
investor rights

orders requiring an official to undertake a specific act). In principle, this forces the investor to choose between the domestic court system and the international one. However, the early cases show that an investor can proceed to an international arbitration after using the domestic courts first, as long as the domestic process is completed, or any (remaining) appeals are waived. If this is done, the investor must then also show as part of its claim that the domestic legal or judicial system has violated the obligations under Chapter 11.[39] Because of this increased burden, the more obvious choice for investors is to use the international process first.

The only remaining constraint on using the arbitration process may be its costs. The practice in international arbitration, unlike domestic court practice, is for the arbitrators and their expenses to be paid by the litigating Parties—costs that can run into the millions of dollars.

7.4   What law is applied by the Tribunal?

The Tribunal is normally called on to interpret and apply the rights of the investor as set out in Chapter 11 of NAFTA. As well, the Tribunal may rule on the more broadly applicable rules of international law. Finally, if the NAFTA Free Trade Commission—composed of the trade ministers of Canada, Mexico and the United States—sets out an interpretation of any provision of Chapter 11 or any other part of NAFTA, the Tribunal must apply that interpretation. This is known in international law as an interpretive statement, and is something that will be returned to later.

It has already been noted that the Tribunals have addressed issues stemming from other parts of NAFTA when making their decisions. While a Tribunal is normally expected to look at specific provisions in the context of the whole agreement to help understand their meaning, it was not anticipated that provisions from the rest of NAFTA would become central to Chapter 11 cases. The extensive reliance on principles of transparency in the *Metalclad* decision, discussed above, is one instance where this has occurred.

As well, it is now open to debate whether other international obligations can be brought into Chapter 11 litigation. As already noted above, some decisions suggest that the breach of an international obligation by a state can be argued by an investor to be a breach of the minimum international standard obligation.

Private Rights,
Public Problems:
A guide to
NAFTA's
controversial
chapter on
investor rights

7.5 Can a Tribunal rule on a country's domestic law?

Can a Tribunal rule on a country's domestic law? At least one Chapter 11 Tribunal, in the *Metalclad v. Mexico* case, went beyond the scope of Chapter 11 and other international law in its decision to do just that. Finding against the expert advice provided by the government of Mexico, it ruled on the constitutional jurisdiction of local governments in Mexico in environmental decision-making.

This part of the *Metalclad* decision, among others, is being challenged in a judicial review of the case. If it is upheld, arbitrators under Chapter 11 will be enabled to rule on the scope and content of a Party's domestic law. While no case can proceed without some understanding of the domestic legal context, the ability of a Chapter 11 Tribunal to issue a ruling on the scope or content of that law is worrying from a basic democratic perspective.

First, there is no requirement for the arbitrators to have any expertise or experience in the domestic law of the Party whose measure is being challenged. Indeed, the arbitration may be their first significant exposure to the law and legal system of the Party in question. Second, the Chapter 11 system has none of the basic safeguards that are now routinely attached to a court of first instance in domestic court systems. In particular, there is little or no public access to the process, and there are limited rights of appeal—two key mechanisms of judicial accountability in the domestic context. If the arbitration process can indeed provide an alternative means to rule on the applicability of domestic law as it applies to major public policy issues, the absence of requirements for experience in that law, and for democratic access and judicial safeguards in the process are serious flaws.

The Chapter 11 system has none of the basic safeguards that are now routinely attached to a court of first instance in domestic court systems. In particular, there is little or no public access to the process, and there are limited rights of appeal.

7.6 The role of previous cases

What role do other cases play? In theory, the decision in one case is not binding on any future Tribunals. Each is legally free to come to its own interpretation. In practice, however, the early decisions of Tribunals on an agreement are extremely important in setting its future direction. Once a trend is established, later Tribunals are more likely to follow this trend than not. This is because certainty is desirable in any legal process, so Tribunals will generally break with such trends only if there are compelling reasons for doing so. As a result, previous cases will always play an important part in practice in a Tribunal's decision-making process, even if they are not legally binding on them.

**Private Rights,
Public Problems:**
A guide to
NAFTA's
controversial
chapter on
investor rights

The absence of a binding role for previous cases—known as a rule of "*stare decisis*" in domestic court systems—is arguably helpful at the moment, given the troubling decisions we have seen to date under Chapter 11. However, in the longer term, there is concern that that the absence of a consistent interpretation of Chapter 11 may lead to the loss of government certainty and public understanding of the obligations governments face.

7.7 How is the public made aware of the cases and their content?

As Box 2 shows, there are two stages to starting an arbitration: the notice of intent to arbitrate that triggers a consultations process, and the actual notice of arbitration. Governments are not legally bound by Chapter 11 to announce, much less release, notices of intent to arbitrate. Indeed, governments have often acted to keep these notices secret,[40] though there are no legal requirements to do so. As a result, there is no guarantee that the known notices of intent to arbitrate listed in Annex 2 actually constitute the full list.

The consequence of secrecy at this stage is important: it provides foreign investors and their companies operating in the host state with privileged but private access to government decision-makers on actual or proposed measures. In effect, the virtually cost-free notice of intent to arbitrate is an exclusive opportunity to lobby, influence, maybe even to threaten, the government on any measure a foreign investor does not like, far from the prying eyes of the public.

The notice of arbitration begins the actual arbitration process. Under Articles 1126(10) and (13), the NAFTA Secretariat must keep a public register of all notices of arbitration. However, the NAFTA Secretariat web site, as of the time of writing, did not set out a public registry of such notices.[41] Further, in the absence of a central office to the NAFTA Secretariat, the three national sections of the NAFTA Secretariat follow different practices in each country. The Canadian office keeps a simple record of the notice being filed, and a key word description of the nature of the claim. The United States office keeps the full notice of arbitration on record and will release copies on request. The Mexican office appears to provide no registry.

More recently, however, the Canadian and U.S. governments have begun to make more information public. In some cases Canada now includes the notice of arbitration and other initial arbitration documents on a public web site.[42] However, this collection was not complete at the time of this writing.

The United States provides access to the notice of arbitration and initial litigation documents in the publicly accessible Reading Room of the U.S. Trade Representative in Washington. As this Guide was being prepared, the U.S. was also in the process of preparing a web site that would contain copies of all the documents in Chapter 11 litigation to which it is a Party. These recent developments are welcome.

Press releases by the foreign investor can also provide information on the starting of arbitration. Another source of information is the ICSID Secretariat web site.[43] When arbitrations are initiated under the ICSID rules, which comprise two of the three sets of rules available under Chapter 11, the case is registered on the web-site, as are updates on the basic procedural status, such as the filing of key written documents or the holding of oral hearings.

Though the NAFTA Parties have recently shown progress on providing public access to documents, at the time of this writing neither the Parties nor any investors had released copies of the actual detailed legal arguments (memorials and counter-memorials, reply and rejoinder), evidence and affidavits in any Chapter 11 case. In the case of the United States, however, the government has apparently now taken the position that association with a Chapter 11 case cannot insulate any documents that could otherwise be discovered through the application of the U.S. *Freedom of Information Act*.[44]

This is something the Parties could be working to change. At least two Chapter 11 cases show that there is nothing in the rules of arbitration that makes these documents confidential. Rather, rules to that effect are established in procedural orders set out by the Tribunals.[45] These orders require the agreement of the governments involved, who are in no way legally bound to agree to an order that requires the secrecy of the arbitration documents. Failure to agree with the foreign investor on the terms of a confidentiality order might leave the issue to be decided by the Tribunal itself. There is no telling how Tribunals would respond to this opportunity, given the growing recognition of the public interest and importance of these cases. At a minimum, government advocacy of public access to all documents would make secrecy more difficult, forcing foreign investors to actually argue against public access to their case, and forcing arbitrators to deny public access.[46]

At a minimum, government advocacy of public access to all documents would make secrecy more difficult, forcing foreign investors to actually argue against public access to their case, and forcing arbitrators to deny public access.

Canada and the United States have expressly stated their intention to publish decisions in Chapter 11 cases, and have done so. Mexico has reserved the right to maintain awards as

**Private Rights,
Public Problems:**
A guide to
NAFTA's
controversial
chapter on
investor rights

confidential, but to date has provided prompt public access to any final awards. Access to any procedural decisions in the cases with Mexico has been very restricted, however. While all final awards and several procedural awards are now available on private web sites,[47] there is still no central government or NAFTA Secretariat site available for this purpose.

7.8 Can the public participate in the process?

The investor-state process is modeled after private commercial arbitration procedures—procedures designed to protect the commercial privacy of the litigants. The result is a Chapter 11 process that excludes guarantees of public participation and in which secrecy is the guiding principle.

NAFTA governments have shown, to varying degrees, an increased willingness to make key documents from Chapter 11 cases available to the public. But, with one exception (discussed below), public participation in the process remains limited to irregular and discretionary after-the-fact access to some, but so far not all, of the formal arbitration documents.

The exception, recently won, is the potential for representatives of civil society to gain access to Chapter 11 arbitrations as "*amici curiae*" or "friends of the court." In many court proceedings in Canada, the United States, and numerous other countries, public participation is allowed through this mechanism. As a result of a recent ruling there is now a real opportunity for this kind of public participation under Chapter 11, though at the discretion of the Tribunal involved.

In the *Methanex* case, the Tribunal was asked first by one Canadian non-governmental organization and subsequently by a coalition of U.S. groups for permission to intervene as "*amici.*" While the Tribunal, at the time of writing, had not actually accepted this request, it had issued a decision stating clearly that it had the ability to do so, a position that was opposed by Mexico and by Methanex itself, but supported by Canada and the United States. As a result, limited public access to present arguments in writing to the Tribunal may now be available in other cases as well. The full range of documents for this important precedent is available on the Internet.[48]

The *amicus* process, however, has its limits as a mechanism for public participation. Importantly, the actual ability to participate remains purely at the discretion of the Tribunal on a case-by-case basis. If admitted, it remains uncertain whether

**Private Rights,
Public Problems:**
A guide to
NAFTA's
controversial
chapter on
investor rights

amici will be granted full access even to arbitration
documents (not to mention hearings). And it is possible that
amici will be subject to "confidentiality orders" by Tribunals
wishing to forbid broader public disclosure of the arbitration
proceedings. To date, there is no agreed code or process for
public participation. Canada did suggest in its submission to
the *Methanex* Tribunal that such a code should be developed
by the NAFTA Parties.

Public access to the actual arbitration hearings is another
issue. Here, the public remains completely shut out to date.
The one Tribunal faced directly with a request for public
access has specifically ruled that this can only be granted with
the express approval of both the arbitrating Parties.[49] This
maintains the historic privacy of arbitration proceedings,
despite the changed nature of the reach of the process. And it
invites the obvious comparison to domestic court
proceedings, all of which are open, raising the question why
the NAFTA governments negotiated an agreement with such a
process attached to it. There is no inherent reason, other than
outdated history, for such secrecy. In any event, the three
NAFTA Parties can seek to promote public access to the
proceedings by asking the Tribunal to allow it. However, as
seen in the *Methanex* case, Tribunals will not likely open the
process without agreement from the private company
involved. This absence of transparency is another way in
which the Chapter 11 process lacks appropriate democratic
safeguards and, therefore, public legitimacy.

7.9   Can a decision be appealed?

There is no appeal of the decision of the Tribunal, a fact that
has provoked strong criticism from non-governmental
groups. In the absence of a proper appeal process, such as that
now seen in the WTO trade law cases, the only avenue open
to the losing Party is to challenge the arbitral award in the
courts of the country where the Tribunal was legally located.
The *Metalclad v. Mexico* and *S.D. Myers v. Canada* cases were
undergoing review by Canadian courts while this guide was in
preparation.[50]

Every arbitration is given a legal location by an order of the
Tribunal. (The *Metalclad* case was officially located in
Vancouver, and the *S.D. Myers* case in Toronto.) Judicial
review is only available in this location in each given case, and
then only to the extent provided by legislation in that
jurisdiction. In any case, the bar set by applicable statutes is
historically very high. Unlike domestic court cases, the
standard of review for arbitrations is not simply whether
there was an error in law in the decision. Rather, it is whether

**Private Rights,
Public Problems:**
A guide to
NAFTA's
controversial
chapter on
investor rights

the error is so big as to amount to a Tribunal acting outside its jurisdiction and in this way negating its own authority to reach a decision that is enforceable. In the two pending appeals, somewhat different standards of review are being sought. How the courts rule on this critical issue will be an important part of the Chapter 11 story.

7.10 Summary

In addition to the substantive concerns over the scope and imbalance of the obligations in Chapter 11, it is clear that the procedure surrounding the investor-state process is one-sided, lacks transparency and does not have the safeguards to the public provided by domestic court processes. Further, the basic legitimacy of the process is challenged by the ability of foreign investors to bypass local laws and legal processes in favor of the international rights and processes domestic businesses do not enjoy. Add to this the potential ability to litigate domestic legal issues in the Chapter 11 process rather than in domestic courts, and the absence of appeals from such decisions, and it becomes apparent that the combined set of problems identified with the Chapter 11 investor-state process is far greater than the sum of its parts.

*The investor-state
process as
currently designed
and implemented
is shockingly
unsuited to the
task of balancing
private rights
against public
goods in a
legitimate and
constructive
manner.*

There is no apparent need for such shortcomings, and little apparent benefit to them. In short, the investor-state process as currently designed and implemented is shockingly unsuited to the task of balancing private rights against public goods in a legitimate and constructive manner.

Valid arguments can be made for providing public access to dispute resolution process to enforce international law. Indeed, in many other areas of international law, such access is available in different forms and expansions of this approach are actively encouraged by civil society organizations and academics. The real issue is to match an appropriate and genuinely accessible process to the nature and scope of the issues that may arise for adjudication. On this level, the investor-state process in Chapter 11 fails, unequivocally.

Endnotes

**Private Rights,
Public Problems:**
A guide to
NAFTA's
controversial
chapter on
investor rights

38 These processes are the International Centre for the Settlement of Investment Disputes (ICSID), to which both national Parties must belong for an investor of one state to sue the host state; the ICSID Additional Facility, which allows its use when only the home or host state is a Party to its rules; and the United Nations Centre For International Trade Law (UNCITRAL), created within the United Nation system. Each has its own rules of procedure, which are applied once the facility is chosen by the investor, unless they are modified in the text of NAFTA itself.

39 This point is made clear in the decision of the Tribunal in *Robert Azinian et al v. Mexico*, of 1999. See Annex 2.

40 For example, the second major notice of intent in an environment-related case in Canada was filed just a day after the *Ethyl* case was settled in July, 1998. However, it was not made public until over a month later, and then only as a result of specific questions asked of government officials by participants in a briefing meeting on the Multilateral Agreement on Investment negotiations.

41 See http://www.nafta-sec-alena.org/.

42 See http://www.dfait-maeci.gc.ca/tna-nac/NAFTA-e.asp.

43 See http://www.worldbank.org/icsid/cases/cases.htm.

44 To the best of our knowledge this position has now been acted upon at least once, following an application for release of specific documents in the *Methanex* case.

45 *S.D. Myers* Procedural Order No. 16, (*In a NAFTA Arbitration Under the UNCITRAL Arbitration Rules Between S.D. Myers v. Canada) 13 May 2000*, paras. 8–9; *Metalclad v. Mexico*, Final award, para. 13; And in *Methanex v. United States*, Decision of the Tribunal on Petitions from Third Persons to Intervene as "*Amici Curiae*," paras. 43–46, the Tribunal states after hinting in a direction against any rule on public access to documents that the matter need not be decided by them due to the Procedural order on confidentiality agreed upon by the Parties in that case.

46 The United States in the ongoing *Methanex v. United States* case did take the step of noting in the Confidentiality Order that documents in that arbitration may be released pursuant to applicable laws, in this case the U.S. *Freedom of Information Act*. See *Methanex v. United States*, Procedural Order 1, para. 2.

47 See http://www.naftaclaims.com/.

48 See the web site of the International Institute for Sustainable Development for the original petitions, subsequent arguments for and against the petitions, and the final decision of the tribunal. http://www.iisd.org/trade/investment_regime.htm. By way of disclosure, IISD was the Canadian NGO that initiated the petition for *amicus* status. The author was and is Counsel to the IISD for this process.

**Private Rights,
Public Problems:**
A guide to
NAFTA's
controversial
chapter on
investor rights

49 *Methanex v. United States,* Decision of the Tribunal on Petitions from Third Persons to Intervene as *"Amici Curiae,"* para. 42.

50 *The United Mexican States v. Metalclad Corporation, (In the Supreme Court of British Columbia: Re Sections 30, 31, and 42 of the Commercial Arbitration Act, R.S.B.C. 1996 C.55 or, in the Alternative section 34 of the International Commercial Arbitration Act, R.S.B.C. 1996 C. 233 AND In the Matter of an Arbitration Pursuant to Chapter Eleven of the North American Free Trade Agreement between Metalclad Corporation and The United Mexican States),* Supreme Court of British Columbia, No. L002904, Vancouver Registry; *Attorney General of Canada v. S.D. Myers,* (In the Matter of Sections 5 and 6 of the Commercial Arbitration Act, R.S.C. 1985 C.17 (2nd Supp.) and in the Matter of an Arbitration under Chapter 11 of the North American Free Trade Agreement Between S.D. Myers and the Government of Canada), Notice of Application, Federal Court, Trial Division, Ottawa, Ontario, Court File T-225-01, February 8, 2001.

8.

Where to now?

**Private Rights,
Public Problems:**
A guide to
NAFTA's
controversial
chapter on
investor rights

The foregoing discussion establishes that neither the substance nor the procedure of Chapter 11 is functioning in a way that is consistent with the goal of sustainable development. Whether the problems result from the "unintended consequences" of using previously innocuous rules in a new international context or from intentional (but unbalanced) policies, the need for reform is equally strong.

The most immediate way NAFTA governments can act to address the problems of Chapter 11 would be to issue a formal "interpretive statement" as allowed under NAFTA Article 1131(2). Such a statement, if adopted by the three Parties acting as the Free Trade Commission, would bind all future Chapter 11 Tribunals.[51] A draft example of an appropriate interpretive statement might look like was developed by the International Institute for Sustainable Development in 1999.[52] While some government discussions on this approach did take place in 1998–1999, they did not get far, and no discussions had been held since the end of 1999. However, as noted above, an attempt to restart the discussions on such a statement has been spearheaded by Canada and appears to have at least the initial support of Mexico and the United States.

Given the mix of substantive and procedural issues, however, it is not clear that an interpretive statement will be sufficient to address all the concerns that have materialized to date. In particular, the democratic deficiencies of Chapter 11 cannot be easily offset within the confines of the current NAFTA text. But suggestions that NAFTA's text be reopened have met with strong resistance from governments who fear the potential for a wholesale renegotiation. Given these fears, governments have two basic options (assuming the *status quo* is not on). First, governments could develop the mutually evident political will to open the Chapter 11 text only so far as required to amend its procedural rules, while developing an interpretive statement in a separate exercise. Formal terms of reference for such a negotiation could easily be crafted, and in any case no government could ever be forced to accept amendments not to its liking. Such negotiations could also take place within any future regional talks destined to supercede NAFTA. Today, governments point to public pressures against NAFTA in general as an excuse for refusing to subject the text to a potentially destabilizing process. But a

**Private Rights,
Public Problems:**
A guide to
NAFTA's
controversial
chapter on
investor rights

*A frank
confrontation of
Chapter 11's
obvious flaws
could only serve to
improve public
confidence in the
system.*

frank confrontation of Chapter 11's obvious flaws could only serve to improve public confidence in the system.

Second—and essentially risk free—governments have the option to move aggressively to promote public access to Chapter 11 cases. They can act, unilaterally or in concert, to pursue maximum release of documents. They can push for open hearings, or at a minimum for prompt release of transcripts. They can aggressively support public participation in *amicus* processes, as the United States and Canada already have. There is no rule of law or procedure that prevents a government taking such steps. If all three were to do so routinely, the chances of a culture of transparency growing around these processes would significantly improve.

8.1   Lessons for other negotiations

*Nearly as urgent as
the need to reform
the operation of
Chapter 11 itself is
the need to ensure
that NAFTA's
investment rules
do not serve as a
template for future
investment
agreements.*

Nearly as urgent as the need to reform the operation of Chapter 11 itself is the need to ensure that NAFTA's investment rules do not serve as a template for future investment agreements. NAFTA's investment provisions, and their investor-state dispute settlement procedure, have opened a Pandora's box of issues concerning the role of private actors in international agreements and the maintenance of the rule of law in a world characterized by globalization. It will ultimately be necessary to devise institutions at the international level that can ensure the kinds of checks and balances that are essential for the pursuit of sustainable development.

The negotiation of other investment regimes, especially in the context of broad regional or global trade agreements, obviously, needs to be carefully considered. Currently, the two most active processes in this area are in the proposed Free Trade Area of the Americas and in calls for including new investment rules within the World Trade Organization system. At present, a number of countries are on record opposing, or at least voicing strong doubts about pursuing investment rules at the WTO.

Several factors suggest that this opposition is well-warranted. As noted in several places above, some of the problems with legal overreaching under NAFTA Chapter 11 stem from an inappropriate conflation of trade rules with investment rules. Investment and trade in goods are very different kinds of international activity. Investors have much more of the quality of residents and participants in the lives of their host countries. While traders tend to clash with measures imposed at the border, investors are far more likely to brush up against domestic regulatory actions of host states. The potential for tension between public and private interests is thus magnified as we have seen, and the WTO is institutionally incapable of the type of balancing of broad policy objectives that this tension demands. The bottom line is that the WTO is not currently a suitable forum for pursuing a new international investment regime.

In the context of the FTAA, negotiations over new investment rules are already underway, with a broad expectation among governments and business interests that they will form an important part of any ultimate agreement. Here, the questions of language are important, as seen above. But prior to any serious discussion over the fine points of treaty terminology, there is a much more fundamental need for a discussion of what should be the basic objective of an investment agreement. A very strong case can be made that the one-dimensional investor rights objective is no longer appropriate given the kinds of consequences this can lead to. Rather, any new agreement should carefully consider the whole investment process, including its social and environmental dimensions.[53] There is no inherent reason why an international regime on investment should be limited to only the investor-protection and investment liberalization aspects, while ignoring other aspects of investment activity, and every reason from these other perspectives why it should be so expanded.

The one-dimensional investor rights objective is no longer appropriate given the kinds of consequences this can lead to. Rather, any new agreement should carefully consider the whole investment process, including its social and environmental dimensions.

Finally, with over 1,800 bilateral investment agreements now concluded and in force, it is apparent that the interpretations of Chapter 11 create an opportunity for literally hundreds of copycat arbitrations to be started, as it appears might have already occurred.[54] Absent a significant reversal of the trends seen in the first few cases, it is a genie that will be increasingly difficult to put back in the bottle. This may well place an enormous burden on the entire investment law area, and make a coordinated international response imperative. On this point, the next several years will be critical.

Private Rights,
Public Problems:
A guide to
NAFTA's
controversial
chapter on
investor rights

Endnotes

51 See Article 1131(2) for the authority to bind Tribunals with such a statement.

52 Mann and von Moltke, 1999, Annex 2, *supra* at 27.

53 For a special discussion of this issue in the FTAA context see Mann and Araya, 2001, *supra* at 19.

54 The first such case appears to be *Technicas Medioambientales Tecmed, S.A. v. United Mexican States*, Case No. ARB(AF)00/02, International Centre for the Settlement of Investment Disputes (Additional Facility), initiated in September 2000 by a Spanish investor under the Spain-Mexico investment agreement. There is as yet no formal public indication of the factual basis or legal grounds for this arbitration that the author is aware of. Informal sources have indicated, however, that the claim closely parallels the *Metalclad* case.

Annex 1:
Selected Excerpts from NAFTA

Private Rights,
Public Problems:
A guide to
NAFTA's
controversial
chapter on
investor rights

NORTH AMERICAN FREE TRADE AGREEMENT

**Between the Government of Canada, the Government
of the United Mexican States and the Government of
the United States of America, 1992**

PREAMBLE

The Government of Canada, the Government of the United
Mexican States and the Government of the United States of
America, resolved to:

- *STRENGTHEN* the special bonds of friendship and
  cooperation among their nations;

- *CONTRIBUTE* to the harmonious development and
  expansion of world trade and provide a catalyst to broader
  international cooperation;

- *CREATE* an expanded and secure market for the goods and
  services produced in their territories;

- *REDUCE* distortions to trade;

- *ESTABLISH* clear and mutually advantageous rules
  governing their trade;

- *ENSURE* a predictable commercial framework for business
  planning and investment;

- *BUILD* on their respective rights and obligations under the
  General Agreement on Tariffs and Trade and other
  multilateral and bilateral instruments of cooperation;

- *ENHANCE* the competitiveness of their firms in global
  markets;

- *FOSTER* creativity and innovation, and promote trade in
  goods and services that are the subject of intellectual
  property rights;

- *CREATE* new employment opportunities and improve
  working conditions and living standards in their respective
  territories;

- *UNDERTAKE* each of the preceding in a manner
  consistent with environmental protection and
  conservation;

- *PRESERVE* their flexibility to safeguard the public welfare;

**Private Rights,
Public Problems:**
A guide to
NAFTA's
controversial
chapter on
investor rights

- *PROMOTE* sustainable development;

- *STRENGTHEN* the development and enforcement of environmental laws and regulations; and

- *PROTECT*, enhance and enforce basic workers' rights;

Chapter One: Objectives

Article 101: Establishment of the Free Trade Area

The Parties to this Agreement, consistent with Article XXIV of the General Agreement on Tariffs and Trade, hereby establish a free trade area.

Article 102: Objectives

1. The objectives of this Agreement, as elaborated more specifically through its principles and rules, including national treatment, most-favored-nation treatment and transparency, are to:

   (a) eliminate barriers to trade in, and facilitate the cross-border movement of, goods and services between the territories of the Parties;

   (b) promote conditions of fair competition in the free trade area;

   (c) increase substantially investment opportunities in the territories of the Parties;

   (d) provide adequate and effective protection and enforcement of intellectual property rights in each Party's territory;

   (e) create effective procedures for the implementation and application of this Agreement, for its joint administration and for the resolution of disputes; and

   (f) establish a framework for further trilateral, regional and multilateral cooperation to expand and enhance the benefits of this Agreement.

2. The Parties shall interpret and apply the provisions of this Agreement in the light of its objectives set out in paragraph 1 and in accordance with applicable rules of international law.

Chapter Two: General Definitions

Article 201: Definitions of General Application

1. For purposes of this Agreement, unless otherwise specified: measure includes any law, regulation, procedure, requirement or practice;

2. For purposes of this Agreement, unless otherwise specified, a reference to a state or province includes local governments of that state or province.

Chapter Eleven: Investment (selected articles)

Section A - Investment

Article 1101: Scope and Coverage

1. This chapter applies to measures adopted or maintained by a Party relating to:

    (a) investors of another Party;

    (b) investments of investors of another Party in the territory of the Party; and

    (c) with respect to Articles 1106 and 1114, all investments in the territory of the Party.

2. A Party has the right to perform exclusively the economic activities set out in Annex III and to refuse to permit the establishment of investment in such activities.

3. This chapter does not apply to measures adopted or maintained by a Party to the extent that they are covered by Chapter Fourteen (Financial Services).

4. Nothing in this chapter shall be construed to prevent a Party from providing a service or performing a function such as law enforcement, correctional services, income security or insurance, social security or insurance, social welfare, public education, public training, health, and child care, in a manner that is not inconsistent with this chapter.

Article 1102: National Treatment

1. Each Party shall accord to investors of another Party treatment no less favorable than that it accords, in like circumstances, to its own investors with respect to the establishment, acquisition, expansion, management, conduct, operation, and sale or other disposition of investments.

Private Rights,
Public Problems:
A guide to
NAFTA's
controversial
chapter on
investor rights

2. Each Party shall accord to investments of investors of another Party treatment no less favorable than that it accords, in like circumstances, to investments of its own investors with respect to the establishment, acquisition, expansion, management, conduct, operation, and sale or other disposition of investments.

3. The treatment accorded by a Party under paragraphs 1 and 2 means, with respect to a state or province, treatment no less favorable than the most favorable treatment accorded, in like circumstances, by that state or province to investors, and to investments of investors, of the Party of which it forms a part.

4. For greater certainty, no Party may:

   (a) impose on an investor of another Party a requirement that a minimum level of equity in an enterprise in the territory of the Party be held by its nationals, other than nominal qualifying shares for directors or incorporators of corporations; or (b) require an investor of another Party, by reason of its nationality, to sell or otherwise dispose of an investment in the territory of the Party.

Article 1103: Most-Favored-Nation Treatment

1. Each Party shall accord to investors of another Party treatment no less favorable than that it accords, in like circumstances, to investors of any other Party or of a non-Party with respect to the establishment, acquisition, expansion, management, conduct, operation, and sale or other disposition of investments.

2. Each Party shall accord to investments of investors of another Party treatment no less favorable than that it accords, in like circumstances, to investments of investors of any other Party or of a non-Party with respect to the establishment, acquisition, expansion, management, conduct, operation, and sale or other disposition of investments.

Article 1104: Standard of Treatment

Each Party shall accord to investors of another Party and to investments of investors of another Party the better of the treatment required by Articles 1102 and 1103.

Article 1105: Minimum Standard of Treatment

1. Each Party shall accord to investments of investors of another Party treatment in accordance with international law, including fair and equitable treatment and full protection and security.

Private Rights,
Public Problems:
A guide to
NAFTA's
controversial
chapter on
investor rights

2. Without prejudice to paragraph 1 and notwithstanding Article 1108(7) (b), each Party shall accord to investors of another Party, and to investments of investors of another Party, nondiscriminatory treatment with respect to measures it adopts or maintains relating to losses suffered by investments in its territory owing to armed conflict or civil strife.

3. Paragraph 2 does not apply to existing measures relating to subsidies or grants that would be inconsistent with Article 1102 but for Article 1108(7) (b).

Article 1106: Performance Requirements

1. No Party may impose or enforce any of the following requirements, or enforce any commitment or undertaking, in connection with the establishment, acquisition, expansion, management, conduct or operation of an investment of an investor of a Party or of a non-Party in its territory:

   (a) to export a given level or percentage of goods or services;

   (b) to achieve a given level or percentage of domestic content;

   (c) to purchase, use or accord a preference to goods produced or services provided in its territory, or to purchase goods or services from persons in its territory;

   (d) to relate in any way the volume or value of imports to the volume or value of exports or to the amount of foreign exchange inflows associated with such investment;

   (e) to restrict sales of goods or services in its territory that such investment produces or provides by relating such sales in any way to the volume or value of its exports or foreign exchange earnings;

   (f) to transfer technology, a production process or other proprietary knowledge to a person in its territory, except when the requirement is imposed or the commitment or undertaking is enforced by a court, administrative tribunal or competition authority to remedy an alleged violation of competition laws or to act in a manner not inconsistent with other provisions of this Agreement; or (g) to act as the exclusive supplier of the goods it produces or services it provides to a specific region or world market.

Private Rights,
Public Problems:
A guide to
NAFTA's
controversial
chapter on
investor rights

2. A measure that requires an investment to use a technology to meet generally applicable health, safety or environmental requirements shall not be construed to be inconsistent with paragraph 1(f). For greater certainty, Articles 1102 and 1103 apply to the measure.

3. No Party may condition the receipt or continued receipt of an advantage, in connection with an investment in its territory of an investor of a Party or of a non-Party, on compliance with any of the following requirements:

   (a) to achieve a given level or percentage of domestic content;

   (b) to purchase, use or accord a preference to goods produced in its territory, or to purchase goods from producers in its territory;

   (c) to relate in any way the volume or value of imports to the volume or value of exports or to the amount of foreign exchange inflows associated with such investment; or

   (d) to restrict sales of goods or services in its territory that such investment produces or provides by relating such sales in any way to the volume or value of its exports or foreign exchange earnings.

4. Nothing in paragraph 3 shall be construed to prevent a Party from conditioning the receipt or continued receipt of an advantage, in connection with an investment in its territory of an investor of a Party or of a non-Party, on compliance with a requirement to locate production, provide a service, train or employ workers, construct or expand particular facilities, or carry out research and development, in its territory.

5. Paragraphs 1 and 3 do not apply to any requirement other than the requirements set out in those paragraphs.

6. Provided that such measures are not applied in an arbitrary or unjustifiable manner, or do not constitute a disguised restriction on international trade or investment, nothing in paragraph 1(b) or (c) or 3(a) or (b) shall be construed to prevent any Party from adopting or maintaining measures, including environmental measures:

   (a) necessary to secure compliance with laws and regulations that are not inconsistent with the provisions of this Agreement;

   (b) necessary to protect human, animal or plant life or health; or

**Private Rights,
Public Problems:**
A guide to
NAFTA's
controversial
chapter on
investor rights

(c) necessary for the conservation of living or non-living exhaustible natural resources.

Article 1107: Senior Management and Boards of Directors

1. No Party may require that an enterprise of that Party that is an investment of an investor of another Party appoint to senior management positions individuals of any particular nationality.

2. A Party may require that a majority of the board of directors, or any committee thereof, of an enterprise of that Party that is an investment of an investor of another Party, be of a particular nationality, or resident in the territory of the Party, provided that the requirement does not materially impair the ability of the investor to exercise control over its investment.

Article 1108: Reservations and Exceptions

1. Articles 1102, 1103, 1106 and 1107 do not apply to:

   (a) any existing nonconforming measure that is maintained by

       (i) a Party at the federal level, as set out in its Schedule to Annex I or III, (ii) a state or province, for two years after the date of entry into force of this Agreement, and thereafter as set out by a Party in its Schedule to Annex I in accordance with paragraph 2, or

       (iii) a local government;

   (b) the continuation or prompt renewal of any nonconforming measure referred to in subparagraph (a); or

   (c) an amendment to any nonconforming measure referred to in subparagraph (a) to the extent that the amendment does not decrease the conformity of the measure, as it existed immediately before the amendment, with Articles 1102, 1103, 1106 and 1107.

2. Each Party may set out in its Schedule to Annex I, within two years of the date of entry into force of this Agreement, any existing non-conforming measure maintained by a state or province, not including a local government.

3. Articles 1102, 1103, 1106 and 1107 do not apply to any measure that a Party adopts or maintains with respect to sectors, subsectors or activities, as set out in its Schedule to Annex II.

Private Rights,
Public Problems:
A guide to
NAFTA's
controversial
chapter on
investor rights

4. No Party may, under any measure adopted after the date of entry into force of this Agreement and covered by its Schedule to Annex II, require an investor of another Party, by reason of its nationality, to sell or otherwise dispose of an investment existing at the time the measure becomes effective.

5. Articles 1102 and 1103 do not apply to any measure that is an exception to, or derogation from, the obligations under Article 1703 (Intellectual Property—National Treatment) as specifically provided for in that Article.

6. Article 1103 does not apply to treatment accorded by a Party pursuant to agreements, or with respect to sectors, set out in its Schedule to Annex IV.

7. Articles 1102, 1103 and 1107 do not apply to:

   (a) procurement by a Party or a state enterprise; or

   (b) subsidies or grants provided by a Party or a state enterprise, including government-supported loans, guarantees and insurance.

8. The provisions of:

   (a) Article 1106(1) (a), (b) and (c), and (3) (a) and (b) do not apply to qualification requirements for goods or services with respect to export promotion and foreign aid programs;

   (b) Article 1106(1) (b), (c), (f) and (g), and (3) (a) and (b) do not apply to procurement by a Party or a state enterprise; and

   (c) Article 1106(3) (a) and (b) do not apply to requirements imposed by an importing Party relating to the content of goods necessary to qualify for preferential tariffs or preferential quotas.

Article 1109: Transfers

1. Each Party shall permit all transfers relating to an investment of an investor of another Party in the territory of the Party to be made freely and without delay. Such transfers include:

   (a) profits, dividends, interest, capital gains, royalty payments, management fees, technical assistance and other fees, returns in kind and other amounts derived from the investment;

(b) proceeds from the sale of all or any part of the investment or from the partial or complete liquidation of the investment;

(c) payments made under a contract entered into by the investor, or its investment, including payments made pursuant to a loan agreement;

(d) payments made pursuant to Article 1110; and

(e) payments arising under Section B.

2. Each Party shall permit transfers to be made in a freely usable currency at the market rate of exchange prevailing on the date of transfer with respect to spot transactions in the currency to be transferred.

3. No Party may require its investors to transfer, or penalize its investors that fail to transfer, the income, earnings, profits or other amounts derived from, or attributable to, investments in the territory of another Party.

4. Notwithstanding paragraphs 1 and 2, a Party may prevent a transfer through the equitable, nondiscriminatory and good faith application of its laws relating to:

(a) bankruptcy, insolvency or the protection of the rights of creditors;

(b) issuing, trading or dealing in securities;

(c) criminal or penal offenses;

(d) reports of transfers of currency or other monetary instruments; or

(e) ensuring the satisfaction of judgments in adjudicatory proceedings.

5. Paragraph 3 shall not be construed to prevent a Party from imposing any measure through the equitable, nondiscriminatory and good faith application of its laws relating to the matters set out in subparagraphs (a) through (e) of paragraph 4.

6. Notwithstanding paragraph 1, a Party may restrict transfers of returns in kind in circumstances where it could otherwise restrict such transfers under this Agreement, including as set out in paragraph 4.

Article 1110: Expropriation and Compensation

1. No Party may directly or indirectly nationalize or expropriate an investment of an investor of another Party in its territory or take a measure tantamount to

**Private Rights,
Public Problems:**
A guide to
NAFTA's
controversial
chapter on
investor rights

nationalization or expropriation of such an investment ("expropriation"), except:

(a) for a public purpose;

(b) on a nondiscriminatory basis;

(c) in accordance with due process of law and Article 1105(1); and

(d) on payment of compensation in accordance with paragraphs 2 through 6.

2. Compensation shall be equivalent to the fair market value of the expropriated investment immediately before the expropriation took place ("date of expropriation"), and shall not reflect any change in value occurring because the intended expropriation had become known earlier. Valuation criteria shall include going concern value, asset value including declared tax value of tangible property, and other criteria, as appropriate, to determine fair market value.

3. Compensation shall be paid without delay and be fully realizable.

4. If payment is made in a G7 currency, compensation shall include interest at a commercially reasonable rate for that currency from the date of expropriation until the date of actual payment.

5. If a Party elects to pay in a currency other than a G7 currency, the amount paid on the date of payment, if converted into a G7 currency at the market rate of exchange prevailing on that date, shall be no less than if the amount of compensation owed on the date of expropriation had been converted into that G7 currency at the market rate of exchange prevailing on that date, and interest had accrued at a commercially reasonable rate for that G7 currency from the date of expropriation until the date of payment.

6. On payment, compensation shall be freely transferable as provided in Article 1109.

7. This Article does not apply to the issuance of compulsory licenses granted in relation to intellectual property rights, or to the revocation, limitation or creation of intellectual property rights, to the extent that such issuance, revocation, limitation or creation is consistent with Chapter Seventeen (Intellectual Property).

8. For purposes of this Article and for greater certainty, a non-discriminatory measure of general application shall

not be considered a measure tantamount to an expropriation of a debt security or loan covered by this chapter solely on the ground that the measure imposes costs on the debtor that cause it to default on the debt.

Article 1114: Environmental Measures

1. Nothing in this chapter shall be construed to prevent a Party from adopting, maintaining or enforcing any measure otherwise consistent with this chapter that it considers appropriate to ensure that investment activity in its territory is undertaken in a manner sensitive to environmental concerns.

2. The Parties recognize that it is inappropriate to encourage investment by relaxing domestic health, safety or environmental measures. Accordingly, a Party should not waive or otherwise derogate from, or offer to waive or otherwise derogate from, such measures as an encouragement for the establishment, acquisition, expansion or retention in its territory of an investment of an investor. If a Party considers that another Party has offered such an encouragement, it may request consultations with the other Party and the two Parties shall consult with a view to avoiding any such encouragement.

Section B - Settlement of Disputes between a Party and an Investor of Another Party

Article 1115: Purpose

Without prejudice to the rights and obligations of the Parties under Chapter Twenty (Institutional Arrangements and Dispute Settlement Procedures), this Section establishes a mechanism for the settlement of investment disputes that assures both equal treatment among investors of the Parties in accordance with the principle of international reciprocity and due process before an impartial tribunal.

Article 1116: Claim by an Investor of a Party on Its Own Behalf

1. An investor of a Party may submit to arbitration under this Section a claim that another Party has breached an obligation under:

   (a) Section A or Article 1503(2) (State Enterprises), or

   (b) Article 1502(3) (a) (Monopolies and State Enterprises) where the monopoly has acted in a manner inconsistent with the Party's obligations under Section A, and that the investor has incurred loss or damage by reason of, or arising out of, that breach.

**Private Rights,
Public Problems:**
A guide to
NAFTA's
controversial
chapter on
investor rights

2. An investor may not make a claim if more than three years have elapsed from the date on which the investor first acquired, or should have first acquired, knowledge of the alleged breach and knowledge that the investor has incurred loss or damage.

Article 1117: Claim by an Investor of a Party on Behalf of an Enterprise

1. An investor of a Party, on behalf of an enterprise of another Party that is a juridical person that the investor owns or controls directly or indirectly, may submit to arbitration under this Section a claim that the other Party has breached an obligation under:

   (a) Section A or Article 1503(2) (State Enterprises), or

   (b) Article 1502(3) (a) (Monopolies and State Enterprises) where the monopoly has acted in a manner inconsistent with the Party's obligations under Section A, and that the enterprise has incurred loss or damage by reason of, or arising out of, that breach.

2. An investor may not make a claim on behalf of an enterprise described in paragraph 1 if more than three years have elapsed from the date on which the enterprise first acquired, or should have first acquired, knowledge of the alleged breach and knowledge that the enterprise has incurred loss or damage.

3. Where an investor makes a claim under this Article and the investor or a non-controlling investor in the enterprise makes a claim under Article 1116 arising out of the same events that gave rise to the claim under this Article, and two or more of the claims are submitted to arbitration under Article 1120, the claims should be heard together by a Tribunal established under Article 1126, unless the Tribunal finds that the interests of a disputing Party would be prejudiced thereby.

4. An investment may not make a claim under this Section.

Article 1118: Settlement of a Claim through Consultation and Negotiation

The disputing Parties should first attempt to settle a claim through consultation or negotiation.

Article 1119: Notice of Intent to Submit a Claim to Arbitration

The disputing investor shall deliver to the disputing Party written notice of its intention to submit a claim to arbitration at least 90 days before the claim is submitted, which notice shall specify:

**Private Rights,
Public Problems:**
A guide to
NAFTA's
controversial
chapter on
investor rights

(a) the name and address of the disputing investor and, where a claim is made under Article 1117, the name and address of the enterprise;

(b) the provisions of this Agreement alleged to have been breached and any other relevant provisions;

(c) the issues and the factual basis for the claim; and

(d) the relief sought and the approximate amount of damages claimed.

Article 1120: Submission of a Claim to Arbitration

1. Except as provided in Annex 1120.1, and provided that six months have elapsed since the events giving rise to a claim, a disputing investor may submit the claim to arbitration under:

(a) the ICSID Convention, provided that both the disputing Party and the Party of the investor are Parties to the Convention;

(b) the Additional Facility Rules of ICSID, provided that either the disputing Party or the Party of the investor, but not both, is a Party to the ICSID Convention; or

(c) the UNCITRAL Arbitration Rules.

2. The applicable arbitration rules shall govern the arbitration except to the extent modified by this Section.

Article 1121: Conditions Precedent to Submission of a Claim to Arbitration

1. A disputing investor may submit a claim under Article 1116 to arbitration only if:

(a) the investor consents to arbitration in accordance with the procedures set out in this Agreement; and

(b) the investor and, where the claim is for loss or damage to an interest in an enterprise of another Party that is a juridical person that the investor owns or controls directly or indirectly, the enterprise, waive their right to initiate or continue before any administrative tribunal or court under the law of any Party, or other dispute settlement procedures, any proceedings with respect to the measure of the disputing Party that is alleged to be a breach referred to in Article 1116, except for proceedings for injunctive, declaratory or other extraordinary relief, not involving the payment of damages, before an administrative tribunal or court under the law of the disputing Party.

**Private Rights,
Public Problems:**
A guide to
NAFTA's
controversial
chapter on
investor rights

2. A disputing investor may submit a claim under Article 1117 to arbitration only if both the investor and the enterprise:

   (a) consent to arbitration in accordance with the procedures set out in this Agreement; and

   (b) waive their right to initiate or continue before any administrative tribunal or court under the law of any Party, or other dispute settlement procedures, any proceedings with respect to the measure of the disputing Party that is alleged to be a breach referred to in Article 1117, except for proceedings for injunctive, declaratory or other extraordinary relief, not involving the payment of damages, before an administrative tribunal or court under the law of the disputing Party.

3. A consent and waiver required by this Article shall be in writing, shall be delivered to the disputing Party and shall be included in the submission of a claim to arbitration.

4. Only where a disputing Party has deprived a disputing investor of control of an enterprise:

   (a) a waiver from the enterprise under paragraph 1(b) or 2(b) shall not be required; and

   (b) Annex 1120.1(b) shall not apply.

Article 1122: Consent to Arbitration

1. Each Party consents to the submission of a claim to arbitration in accordance with the procedures set out in this Agreement.

2. The consent given by paragraph 1 and the submission by a disputing investor of a claim to arbitration shall satisfy the requirement of:

   (a) Chapter II of the ICSID Convention (Jurisdiction of the Centre) and the Additional Facility Rules for written consent of the Parties;

   (b) Article II of the New York Convention for an agreement in writing; and

   (c) Article I of the Inter-American Convention for an agreement.

Article 1123: Number of Arbitrators and Method of Appointment

Except in respect of a Tribunal established under Article 1126, and unless the disputing Parties otherwise agree, the Tribunal

**Private Rights,
Public Problems:**
A guide to
NAFTA's
controversial
chapter on
investor rights

shall comprise three arbitrators, one arbitrator appointed by each of the disputing Parties and the third, who shall be the presiding arbitrator, appointed by agreement of the disputing Parties.

Article 1124: Constitution of a Tribunal When a Party Fails to Appoint an Arbitrator or the Disputing Parties Are Unable to Agree on a Presiding Arbitrator

1. The Secretary-General shall serve as appointing authority for an arbitration under this Section.

2. If a Tribunal, other than a Tribunal established under Article 1126, has not been constituted within 90 days from the date that a claim is submitted to arbitration, the Secretary-General, on the request of either disputing Party, shall appoint, in his discretion, the arbitrator or arbitrators not yet appointed, except that the presiding arbitrator shall be appointed in accordance with paragraph 3.

3. The Secretary-General shall appoint the presiding arbitrator from the roster of presiding arbitrators referred to in paragraph 4, provided that the presiding arbitrator shall not be a national of the disputing Party or a national of the Party of the disputing investor. In the event that no such presiding arbitrator is available to serve, the Secretary-General shall appoint, from the ICSID Panel of Arbitrators, a presiding arbitrator who is not a national of any of the Parties.

4. On the date of entry into force of this Agreement, the Parties shall establish, and thereafter maintain, a roster of 45 presiding arbitrators meeting the qualifications of the Convention and rules referred to in Article 1120 and experienced in international law and investment matters. The roster members shall be appointed by consensus and without regard to nationality.

Article 1125: Agreement to Appointment of Arbitrators

For purposes of Article 39 of the ICSID Convention and Article 7 of Schedule C to the ICSID Additional Facility Rules, and without prejudice to an objection to an arbitrator based on Article 1124(3) or on a ground other than nationality:

(a) the disputing Party agrees to the appointment of each individual member of a Tribunal established under the ICSID Convention or the ICSID Additional Facility Rules;

(b) a disputing investor referred to in Article 1116 may submit a claim to arbitration, or continue a claim, under the ICSID Convention or the ICSID Additional

Private Rights,
Public Problems:
A guide to
NAFTA's
controversial
chapter on
investor rights

Facility Rules, only on condition that the disputing investor agrees in writing to the appointment of each individual member of the Tribunal; and

(c) a disputing investor referred to in Article 1117(1) may submit a claim to arbitration, or continue a claim, under the ICSID Convention or the ICSID Additional Facility Rules, only on condition that the disputing investor and the enterprise agree in writing to the appointment of each individual member of the Tribunal.

Article 1130: Place of Arbitration

Unless the disputing Parties agree otherwise, a Tribunal shall hold an arbitration in the territory of a Party that is a Party to the New York Convention, selected in accordance with:

(a) the ICSID Additional Facility Rules if the arbitration is under those Rules or the ICSID Convention; or

(b) the UNCITRAL Arbitration Rules if the arbitration is under those Rules.

Article 1131: Governing Law

1. A Tribunal established under this Section shall decide the issues in dispute in accordance with this Agreement and applicable rules of international law.

2. An interpretation by the Commission of a provision of this Agreement shall be binding on a Tribunal established under this Section.

**Private Rights,
Public Problems:**
A guide to
NAFTA's
controversial
chapter on
investor rights

Annex 2:
Digest of known Chapter 11
cases, 1994–2000

Documents referred to in this digest are available now on a
combination of governmental and non-governmental
Internet sites. See www.naftalaw.org, www.state.gov,
www.dfait-maeci.gc.ca/tna-nac/NAFTA-e.asp and
www.iisd.org/trade/investment_regime.htm The U.S.
government site was not up and running at the time of this
writing, but was anticipated to be in operation shortly. All
final decisions are available on one or more of these sites, and
for some cases many more documents are available as well.
For other cases there is virtually nothing at this time.

Due to the high proportion and profile of the environment-
related cases, they are reviewed first in this digest. However,
the non-environmental cases are equally important to the full
history of Chapter 11, and are given equal treatment in terms
of their description. At the same time, it may be noted that no
final decisions in this latter group of cases has been issued to
date.

The list of cases is accompanied by the start date and end date
of each case, where a case is now terminated. One case, *Waste
Management v. Mexico*, originally thought terminated in June
2000 has now been recommenced.

The case descriptions are not intended to, and do not, provide
comprehensive legal analysis of the elements of the case. They
seek to provide a general description of the issues raised, how
they were addressed in each case, and potential impacts the
case may have.

This review does not cover the growing number of Tribunal
decisions dealing with confidentiality of documents, location
of the Tribunal, order of the proceedings, access to
government documents, etc. The only procedural issue
covered here is public participation as a friend of the court, as
a result of a major decision on this in the *Methanex* case.

This analysis is based on the facts and decisions as of March 1,
2001, to the best ability of the author.

**Private Rights,
Public Problems:**
A guide to
NAFTA's
controversial
chapter on
investor rights

LIST OF CASES

Environment-related Cases

1. Ethyl Corp. v. Canada, 1996–1998

2. Metalclad v. Mexico, 1996, ongoing

3. Robert Azinian *et al.* (Desona de. C.V.) v. Mexico, 1996–1999

4. Waste Management (Acaverde) v. Mexico, (No. 1), 1998–2000

5. Waste Management (Acaverde) v. Mexico, (No. 2), 2000–ongoing

6. S.D. Myers v. Canada, 1998–ongoing

7. Sun Belt Water v. Canada, 1998, in abeyance

8. Pope & Talbot v. Canada, 1998–ongoing

9. Methanex v. United States, 1998–ongoing

10. Ketchum Investments Inc. and Tysa Investments Inc. v. Canada, 2000–ongoing

Non-Environment Cases

11. Halchette Distribution System v. Mexico, 1995, not pursued

12. Signa S.A. de C.V. v. Canada, 1995, not pursued

13. Marvin Ray Feldman Karpa v. Mexico, 1998–ongoing

14. Loewen Group v. United States, 1998–ongoing

15. Mondev International v. United States, 1999–ongoing

16. U.P.S. v. Canada, 2000–ongoing

17. A.D.F. Group v. United States, 2000–ongoing

**Private Rights,
Public Problems:**
A guide to
NAFTA's
controversial
chapter on
investor rights

1.
Ethyl Corporation v. Canada

Key dates:

Notice of Intent to Arbitrate:	September 10, 1996
Notice of Arbitration:	April 14, 1997
Procedural hearing on jurisdiction:	February, 1998
Decision on Jurisdiction:	June 24, 1998
Canada settles case:	July 20, 1998

The facts

Ethyl Corp. is a U.S. company that established a Canadian subsidiary, Ethyl Canada. The main, but not only, work of Ethyl Canada was to receive methylcyclopentadienyl manganese tricarbonyl (MMT) from its parent company and mix it with other agents for distribution across Canada as a gasoline additive. Use of MMT is banned for environmental reasons in a significant number of U.S. states. Ethyl Corp. is the only manufacturer of MMT in the world and Ethyl Canada was the only mixer in Canada.

In 1997, the Canadian Parliament adopted a law banning the import of MMT into Canada, as well as its inter-provincial trade.[1] Owing to jurisdictional and statutory factors unique to Canada, the law did not directly ban the sale or use of MMT in Canada, leading some to argue the law was discriminatory. However, in practice, the law would have ended any sales or use of MMT since the only source of it, Ethyl Corp. was located in the United States.

Canada banned the import of MMT for two reasons. First, there was concern that manganese, which is part of MMT, has toxic properties that have not been fully assessed by science. Second, there was concern that MMT caused newly required equipment on car exhaust systems to malfunction, which would lead to increased air pollution. In fact, all the North American and major international automobile manufacturers selling in Canada strongly supported the ban.

The investor's claims

Ethyl Corp. claimed $250 million in damages, alleging that at least three breaches had taken place:

- *Article 1102, National Treatment.* Ethyl Corp. claimed the ban on imports, in the absence of a ban on internal production and sale, was a breach of the obligation to treat foreign and domestic investors in a no less favourable

71

**Private Rights,
Public Problems:**
A guide to
NAFTA's
controversial
chapter on
investor rights

manner. This claim was made despite the fact that there was no domestic Canadian production of MMT, and that Ethyl Corp.'s own documents showed it would not be economical to open plants to produce MMT in Canada. Ethyl also claimed the MMT ban was a disguised way to support Canadian-made octane enhancing products.

· *Article 1106, Performance Requirements.* One type of performance requirement forces an investor to use a certain amount or type of domestically-produced goods or services in its production process. Article 1106 bans these types of requirements. Ethyl Corp. claimed the import restriction was an illegal performance requirement, forcing Ethyl Corp. either to produce the MMT in Canada or to use other Canadian-made products instead.

· *Article 1110, Expropriation.* Ethyl Corp. argued that the ban on MMT amounted to an expropriation of its business in Canada or, alternatively, was a measure "tantamount to" expropriation, for which it should be fully compensated. This was the first time this expropriation argument had been made under an investment agreement to challenge an environmental law, and the first time the expansive use of the term measure "tantamount to" expropriation had been used in a legal proceeding.

Award on jurisdiction

Canada had objected to the jurisdiction of the Tribunal to hear the case under Chapter 11, arguing primarily that the MMT law was not a performance requirement under Chapter 11 but a trade measure outside the scope of Chapter 11. A second set of arguments concerned whether there was a "measure" in law at the time the case was initiated, as the MMT legislation had not yet been fully enacted and was not in force. It did come into force subsequently.

On June 24, 1998, the Chapter 11 arbitrators rejected Canada's arguments on both counts. On the issue of whether a trade measure falling under other parts of NAFTA could also be subject to a Chapter 11 proceeding, the Tribunal noted succinctly there was no apparent conflict here in so allowing, and rejected Canada's argument this was outside the Tribunal's jurisdiction (paras. 63–64).

On the issue of whether an Act that has not yet passed into law can be a measure under Chapter 11, the Tribunal noted that Ethyl had initiated its action prematurely, as the Act was not yet in force. Moreover, the Tribunal recognized this was done for "tactical reasons relating to the legislative process," in other words for the purpose of trying to affect the legislative debate in Parliament on the adoption of the MMT law it had consistently opposed (para. 87). Still, the Tribunal found that as the Act had indeed become law shortly afterward, this "jumping the gun" was not significant enough to terminate the jurisdiction of the Tribunal.

In making these rulings, the Tribunal made a specific point of noting that Chapter 11 was not to be strictly construed based on a principle of avoiding restrictions on sovereignty (para. 55).

The settlement of the case

Shortly after the Award on Jurisdiction was issued, Canada "settled" the case. Canada stated that it did so mainly do uphold an unfavorable decision under Canada's Internal Trade Agreement (ITA).

Ironically, the decision in the ITA case expressly said that it was not recommending the withdrawal of the MMT Act. In addition, that case did not address the international import ban at all, focusing instead on the ban on inter-provincial trade. The ITA Panel held the MMT law to be a *bona-fide* environmental law. In other words, it was not a disguised restriction on trade, a protectionist measure or a support for one type of octane enhancer over another. The Panel also found there was sufficient evidence for the government to have acted upon. It also found the process for consultations with the provinces set out in the ITA was not followed sufficiently, and that the inter-provincial trade ban was more trade restrictive than necessary. However, the alternative suggested by the Panel of a two pump system (one for gasoline with MMT and one without) was rejected by the gasoline industry on several occasions, making this an illusory alternative.[2]

In settling the case, Canada:

• paid Ethyl $13 million for costs and lost profits while the Act was in place;

• withdrew the legislation that Ethyl opposed; and

• gave Ethyl a letter to use as it saw fit saying there was no scientific evidence of any health risk of MMT or any impact on car exhaust systems.[3]

What is the impact of the Ethyl case?

As the first environment-related Chapter 11 case, *Ethyl* broke new ground and has led to a number of other cases. Its arguments that environmental legislation could be a breach of the rules on performance requirements and expropriation

Private Rights,
Public Problems:
A guide to
NAFTA's
controversial
chapter on
investor rights

were new, and raised concerns that any foreign-owned corporation could use similar arguments to attack new environmental regulations that impacted its profits. The invocation of Chapter 11 as part of the lobbying process to oppose enactment of legislation was also an important first.

Since it was also the first case to proceed past the Notice of Intent to Arbitrate and actually go to arbitration, the *Ethyl* case set a major precedent when it was settled by Canada.

2.
Metalclad Corp. v. Mexico

Key dates:

Notice of Intent to Arbitrate:	October 2, 1996
Notice of Arbitration:	January 13, 1997
Oral hearings completed:	August 30–September 9, 1999
Final decision:	August 30, 2000
Petition to the Court of British Columbia for Judicial Review and Appeal:	October 27, 2000, ongoing

The facts

The case was brought by Metalclad Corp., a U.S. company in the waste management business, against Mexico. In 1993, Metalclad purchased a Mexican waste management company that operated a waste transfer station in the municipality of Guadalcazar in the hopes of building and operating a full hazardous waste landfill facility on that location. Municipal permits for this purpose had previously been denied to the vendor. A state-level permit was subsequently granted for the construction of the landfill, subject to certain technical requirements being met, but without prejudice to other authorizations that may be required. The federal government in Mexico issued the required permits from that level. Acting on this and on what the Tribunal accepted as assurances by the Mexican government that all permits either were issued or would be issued without a problem, construction was initiated.

No municipal permit was ever received by Metalclad. The Tribunal accepted that Mexican federal officials told Metalclad that municipal permits were not necessary to build or operate the landfill, despite Mexican submissions that no such

**Private Rights,
Public Problems:**
A guide to
NAFTA's
controversial
chapter on
investor rights

assurances were offered. The Tribunal also accepted that Metalclad acted upon these representations. Construction was initiated without a municipal construction permit, and continued until municipal authorities ordered that it stop. Construction resumed when a municipal permit was applied for in November, 1994, and following receipt of additional federal permits. In the meantime, an environmental assessment "confirmed" the site was suitable for a hazardous waste landfill, subject to certain engineering requirements being met. Plans were also required for site remediation work to take place during the first three years of commercial operation. The municipal permit was finally denied in December, 1995, thus ending the final construction and preventing any entry into operation of the landfill site. The Tribunal noted specifically that Metalclad was not notified of the town meeting where the permit was denied, was thus not given a chance to be heard in this meeting, and that their request for a reconsideration was denied. Even after the denial of the municipal permit, federal authorities authorized the ten-fold expansion of the facility.

Finally, in September 1997, the Governor of the state involved issued an Ecological Decree declaring the area in which the landfill site sits to be a natural reserve for the preservation of rare cactus. This Decree effectively foreclosed future use of the site as a landfill.

The investor's claims

Metalclad claimed violations of two main provisions of Chapter 11, Article 1105 on minimum international standards and Article 1110 on expropriation.

The Tribunal's ruling

The Tribunal ruled against Mexico and awarded $16,685,000.00 to Metalclad.

Basis of interpretation of Chapter 11

A key part of the ruling is the selective reference to three NAFTA objectives as underpinnings for the interpretation of Chapter 11. These are:

- Transparency in government regulations and activity (para. 70–71);

- The substantial increase in investment opportunities (para. 70, 75);

- To ensure a predictable commercial framework for investors (para. 71).

**Private Rights,
Public Problems:**
A guide to
NAFTA's
controversial
chapter on
investor rights

In addition, the Tribunal argued there was a general purpose to "ensure the successful implementation of investment initiatives" (para. 75). The entire ruling is predicated on this allocution of underlying principles: that Chapter 11 is for the promotion of investments and investors, indeed, to ensure that they succeed. This ignores the counterbalance included in the preamble to NAFTA relating to environmental protection and sustainable development as equal underlying principles, and clearly suggested an uphill battle for introducing such a balance into future rulings.

Article 1105, Minimum standards of treatment

The Tribunal ruled that Mexico breached its obligation to provide minimum standards of treatment in several ways (paras. 74–100):

- not living up to representations it ruled were made by Federal and State officials that the plant would be able to operate, which it held the investor had a right under NAFTA to rely upon;

- not clarifying understandings of Mexican law (which it ruled the government has an obligation to do if any uncertainty arises for the investor);

- not having clear procedures for investors to easily know the rules on permits, in breach of the transparency obligations in non-Chapter 11 parts of NAFTA;

- ruling, against Mexican government legal experts, that the municipality exceeded its own legal functions by requiring a municipal permit or, if one was required, by extending its reach to the use of the facility;

- ruling that environmental factors were legally only a federal issue and hence could not be used as a basis for denying a municipal permit, since the project had passed federal inspection;

- not notifying Metalclad of the relevant town meeting concerning its permit.

The tribunal summed up its findings by saying that Mexico failed to provide a transparent, predictable framework for business planning and investment, and demonstrated a lack of orderly process and timely disposition in relation to an investor (para. 99).

A critical underpinning of this decision is the ruling by the panel on the scope of environmental authority of municipalities in Mexico, which went against the interpretations provided by Mexico. In effect, almost the entire case turns on the legal finding by the panel that the municipality exceeding its jurisdiction. The rulings against the Mexican interpretations on the substance of Mexican law are troubling, and raise questions about the jurisdiction of the panel and its ability to address such an issue.

Article 1110, Expropriation

- The Tribunal ruled that the same actions that lead to the finding of a breach of Article 1105 also lead to a breach of the rules on expropriation, given that no compensation was paid. This is the first time breaches of process have been analogized to expropriation, and makes the scope of what constitutes an expropriation very unclear. The Tribunal's apparent determination that an act outside the scope of authority of the municipality could itself found an expropriation complaint also raises questions about what limits are available here (paras. 104–107).

- The Tribunal's test for expropriation was solely focused on the extent of the interference with property rights. It further stated that expropriation could include "covert or incidental interference with the use of property" (para. 103).

- The Tribunal went on to apparently rule (there is some doubt on this) that the purpose for a government measure need not be considered in this regard (para. 110).

Transparency of Chapter 11 proceedings:

Paradoxically, given its focus on transparency in the NAFTA, the Tribunal expressly limited transparency in its own proceedings to disclosures required by national law applicable to the litigating Parties. It did so despite its express recognition that there are no legal provisions requiring them to impose such limits. Its basis for doing so was the effective operation of the proceedings (para. 13). This approach has been repeated in subsequent proceedings.

The petition for review and appeal

In October 2000, Mexico initiated a petition to the Supreme Court of British Columbia seeking review of, or appeal from, the Tribunal's ruling.[4] This petition was initiated in British Columbia because the legal location of the Tribunal was in that province (Vancouver). Mexico relied upon two statutes in British Columbia dealing with arbitrations.[5] Such statutes are needed in order to base a claim for review or appeal of an arbitral award, and are a common feature of arbitration practice around the world.

**Private Rights,
Public Problems:**
A guide to
NAFTA's
controversial
chapter on
investor rights

Mexico's petition highlighted the following claims (para. 72 of the Amended Petition of Mexico):

- The Tribunal exceeded its powers (jurisdiction) by:

  – including provisions from other parts of NAFTA as central parts of its legal ruling, thereby "legislating" new Chapter 11 provisions;

  – equating an alleged violation of domestic law to a breach of international law; and

  – arrogating to itself powers to decide issues of Mexican law as if it were a domestic court.

- The Tribunal erred in its interpretations of Article 1105 and 1110 as well as in its interpretation of Mexican law.

- The Tribunal failed to address all the issues it was presented; to fully explain its reasons as required by the Arbitration rules; and to have regard for all the evidence presented.

The petition was heard in February–March, 2001 in Vancouver, B.C. A decision is anticipated sometime in the spring of 2001.

Impacts of the case

The decision as it now stands raises the question: what is the extent of the transparency and other procedural requirements to be accorded to an investor under Article 1105? At an extreme end, they may require governments to act almost as legal advisors to foreign investors, correcting any legal errors they make, and providing to the investor guidance on how to make its investment in an efficient way. In addition, it raises the possibility of representations by officials at one level of government having a binding impact on decisions that legally have to be made by another level of government. This decision raises new areas of uncertainty as regards the application and scope of the minimum international standards provision.

The scope of a Tribunal's ability to rule on domestic law is also important, especially as the Tribunal in this case imposed high levels of secrecy requirements while so ruling.

The combination of establishing a test for expropriation based solely on the significance of the impact on the business, and apparently negating the need to consider the purpose of a measure, creates a most significant problem for environmental law makers. This view, if its stands in other cases, means the effective end of the traditional international law "police powers" limitation on the concept of

Private Rights,
Public Problems:
A guide to
NAFTA's
controversial
chapter on
investor rights

expropriation, which allowed governments to protect the public welfare without compensation, and hence a radical expansion of the pre-existing understanding of the meaning of expropriation in investment agreements. Consequently, any environmental law that interferes with the use of an investment to generate profit could fall within the scope of Article 1110, and require compensation.

The launching of the petition for review or appeal was a very significant Chapter 11 development. It will provide the first indication of relevant standards for reviewing these arbitrations, given their public law aspects. In addition, if no review or appeal is accepted, it will confirm the scope of the findings as within appropriate ranges for Chapter 11.

3.
Robert Azinian et al (Desona de. C.V.) v. Mexico

Key dates:

Notice of Intent to Arbitrate:	December 16, 1996
Notice of Arbitration:	March 10, 1997
Final decision:	November 1, 1999

The facts

The investors based their claim on an alleged breach of a 15-year concession contract to collect garbage in the municipality of Naupalcan, a suburb of Mexico City, signed in 1993. After the municipality questioned the performance of the contract by Desona, the "investment" in Mexico, the company challenged its legal ability to raise the complaints. In March 1994, the municipality cancelled the concession contract for non-performance by Desona. Desona appealed this decision in court, with subsequent judicial appeals up to the Federal Circuit Court. All these legal actions failed. Several aspects of the contract, such as a failure to provide the new waste disposal trucks promised, were upheld as valid grounds for terminating the contract. The investors argued the termination of the contract in this case was a breach of Chapter 11 and sought damages for lost profits. The Tribunal found additional facts:

- The claiming investors had seen the contract in question as an initial foray in a broader plan for seeking waste management opportunities in Mexico. However, they had limited resources to implement the broader plan, and hoped to leverage the contract into a commercial relationship with large operators in the field;

Private Rights,
Public Problems:
A guide to
NAFTA's
controversial
chapter on
investor rights

- Significant false representations had been made by the investors, including the absence of firm commitments from other Parties described as providing financial backing before the contract was signed, and the actual withdrawal of a major partner prior to signing the contract;

- Non-performance of several contract requirements;

- Associated required plans under the contract, such as the construction of a major landfill-connected power plant, were financially and technically impossible; and

- Testimony from some of the investors' witnesses was not truthful.

The investor's claims

The investors sought $19 million in damages, based on the following claims:

- *Article 1105, Minimum international standards of treatment.* Azinian alleged a failure by the municipality to achieve minimum international standards for treatment of foreign investors, but specific details of the claim are not available. (In fact, the panel noted that the ground was barely supported by the investors, and no relevant details or examples of a failure to meet this standard were offered.)

- *Article 1110, Expropriation.* Azinian argued that the cancellation of the contract was an expropriation under Article 1110.

The Tribunal's decision

The consequences of the prior domestic proceedings

The panel did not address the Chapter 11 grounds of the claim in detail. Instead it considered a preliminary question as to whether it had the jurisdiction to address a case where a contract had been ended by a legitimate authority and this had been duly upheld by three levels of courts on appeal.

- The tribunal made it clear that its role was not as an appeals court against the original decision or the decisions of the courts, but to determine whether a breach of NAFTA's Chapter 11 had occurred.

- At the same time the panel made it clear that taking prior action in domestic courts was not a barrier to using the Chapter 11 process (paras. 86, 97 *et seq.*).

- As the administrative decision to cancel the contract was supported by three levels of courts, the panel found that a breach of Chapter 11 would have to be based on a breach of these obligations by the courts themselves. If the courts had acted properly under NAFTA's obligations in upholding the cancellation of the contract, then the cancellation itself could not be a breach.

• The panel found that for a court decision to violate Chapter 11, the investor must show either "a denial of justice or a pretence of form to achieve an internationally unlawful end." A denial of justice was described as arising if the courts refused to entertain a suit, if it was subjected to undue delay or if they administer justice in a seriously inadequate way (paras. 99–104).

No denial of justice or other judicial impropriety was alleged or shown to exist in this case. The panel found that the judicial decisions were based on ample facts, as already described above, to uphold the cancellation of the contract.

Foundation of a Chapter 11 case: breach of Chapter 11

• The panel found the case was essentially one of breach of contract. It ruled that a breach of contract *per se* did not make a case, unless accompanied by a breach of the obligations in Chapter 11. Disappointment or disagreement with an administrative or judicial decision is not the basis for such a breach (para. 83).

• As the investor had not challenged either the underlying law allowing the cancellation of municipal contracts as an expropriation, or the court proceedings that upheld the cancellation, the Tribunal found that the investors had not raised the appropriate issues under Chapter 11, but even if they had they would have failed because the domestic courts' actions met the standards of propriety.

What is the impact of the case?

The decision of the panel appears to be largely based on the facts and the investors' poorly directed legal arguments. Mexico was able to establish that the investors' company misled the authorities about its capacity to perform the contract work and that initial level of performance, itself, provided the proper basis for cancellation of the contract. Mexican actions in this regard, and the subsequent court rulings, were made in good faith and appropriate.

There is nothing in the ruling that directly relates to the legal issues concerning the application of the Chapter 11 provisions on expropriation and national treatment. However, the clear statement that a simple breach of contract does not provide a basis for an international arbitration is important, as is the

**Private Rights,
Public Problems:**
A guide to
NAFTA's
controversial
chapter on
investor rights

requirement to carefully pinpoint the alleged breach of Chapter 11. Also important is the statement that the role of an arbitration panel is not as an appeals court against an administrative decision or the decisions of the domestic courts, but rather is to determine whether a breach of NAFTA's Chapter 11 had occurred. This ruling may help prevent inappropriate uses of the Chapter 11 mechanism.

4.
Waste Management (Acaverde) v. Mexico (No. 1)

Key dates:

Notice of Intent to Arbitrate:	February 29, 1998/ June 30, 1998 (in dispute)
Notice of Arbitration:	November 18, 1998
Final decision:	June 2, 2000

The facts

Although a decision has been issued in this case, it was based on a preliminary question of the jurisdiction of the Tribunal, with a minimal factual record. Consequently, knowledge of the facts remains minimal. Waste Management alleged breach of contract by several state-owned entities and the City of Acapulco in relation to the cancellation of a waste management contract.

The investor's claims

Waste Management claimed $60M on the basis of breaches of Articles 1105 (minimum international standards) and 1110 (expropriation) of Chapter 11.

The jurisdictional issue

Claimants in a Chapter 11 arbitration are required under Article 1121 to waive their rights to pursue domestic legal proceedings relating to the measure(s) addressed in the case. Mexico claimed that Waste Management's waiver in this case did not fully comply with Article 1121's requirements.

The award of the Tribunal

In a 2-1 decision, the Tribunal upheld Mexico's objection to jurisdiction. It ruled that the waiver was insufficient to stop then ongoing proceedings in Mexican courts relating to the same "measure" that led to the Chapter 11 complaint.

**Private Rights,
Public Problems:**
A guide to
NAFTA's
controversial
chapter on
investor rights

- The spirit and intent of the waiver requirement was to prevent duplication of processes involving claims for damages, bearing in mind that a NAFTA claim will address international law issues and a domestic claim domestic law issues, and hence will be based on different legal issues.

- The waiver requirement goes to cases that have a legal basis that is derived from the same measures. Domestic and Chapter 11 cases cannot invoke the same measures as part of their cases (para. 27.b).

- Article 1121 proscribes the initiation or continuation of proceedings in a Party's courts with respect to a measure that is alleged to be a breach of Chapter 11 and subject to a Chapter 11 proceeding (para. 28).

- The waiver in this case contained additional interpretations that failed to translate as an effective abdication of rights mandated by a waiver (para. 31.2).

What is the impact of the case?

The case does highlight the importance of the waiver requirement as the main procedural "hurdle" in the Chapter 11 process. While other Tribunals have been prepared to overlook purely formalistic aspects of the waiver process, such as the exact time it was submitted or an improper signature, this case shows the need to ensure the substantive reach of the waiver is complete. This may help ensure the intent of avoiding duplicative proceedings is met.

5.
Waste Management v. Mexico (No. 2)

Key dates:

Notice of arbitration: September 27, 2000

Ongoing

The facts

This case follows the rejection by the Tribunal of the first Chapter 11 arbitration as discussed previously. There are no public documents at time of writing. The facts are presumed to be the same. According to press reports, Waste Management believes it has corrected the procedural faults with the waiver and concluded all domestic court cases in Mexico, thereby allowing the case to proceed.

Private Rights,
Public Problems:
A guide to
NAFTA's
controversial
chapter on
investor rights

The investor's claims

In the absence of further written documents, we presume here
that the grounds of the case will be the same as in the first case,
namely breaches by Mexico of Articles 1105 and 1110. Press
reports indicate that the claimant intends to rely on the
Metalclad v. Mexico case as an important part of its claim.[6]

The importance of the case

The case highlights the need to distinguish between the
substantive aspects of a decision, upon which a ruling is final,
and the procedural aspects, which may admit of correction
and re-institution of the case. There is no public indication of
Mexican arguments on this possible point at this time.

6.

S. D. Myers v. Canada

Key dates:

Notice of Intent to Arbitrate:	July 22, 1998
Notice of Arbitration:	October 30, 1998
Decision on the merits:	November 13, 2000
Decision on damages pending filing by Canada of Notice of Application for Judicial Review:	February 8, 2001

The facts

On November 20, 1995, the government of Canada imposed a
temporary but comprehensive ban on the export of PCB
wastes to the United States. This was in response to
administrative action taken by the U.S. Environmental
Protection Agency (EPA) following a court decision that
required it to open the border to PCB waste imports from
Canada. The border had been closed to such imports prior to
the court decision. In February 1997, a less comprehensive
but permanent regulation was put in place, allowing PCB
waste exports to certain types of disposal facilities, but not to
any landfill sites. In July 1997, the EPA action opening the
border was overturned by a U.S. Court of Appeal decision,
and the border was closed once again by the U.S. The
Canadian action prevented PCB waste exports from Canada
during this period of legal change in the U.S. They are now,
and were previously, prevented by U.S. law.

The investor, S.D. Myers, is a U.S. hazardous waste disposal
company with offices in Canada, but all its disposal facilities
in the U.S. It had been one of the companies behind the legal

challenges to the closed border in the U.S., and had sought other enforcement discretion through various U.S. administrative processes. The company sought to export PCB wastes from Canada to its U.S. disposal facilities.

The Tribunal noted two facts in particular. The Environment Minister of the day had stated in Parliament that it was the position of the government "that the handling of PCBs should be done in Canada by Canadians" (para. 116, partial award). This was stated to show that the measure had a protectionist intent. The second fact was that Environment Canada officials indicated in briefing material that the export of PCB wastes to the U.S. was not inherently environmentally unsound, and could have environmental benefits.

The investor's claims

S. D. Myers claimed that the denial by Canada of the ability to export PCB wastes to the United States during the window when court action in the U.S. would have allowed this to be done was a breach of Chapter 11 by Canada. The company claimed $20 million for lost profits and opportunities. The claim was based on:

- *Art. 1102, National Treatment.* S.D. Myers claimed Canada shut the border to favor Canadian PCB waste disposers. It also claims that Canada acted despite knowing the investor was a U.S. firm and that its business would be harmed more than others. No Canadian firms were permitted to export PCB waste at the time.

- *Article 1105, Minimum International Standards of Treatment.* S.D. Myers argued that the treatment was neither fair nor equitable, and constituted a denial of justice, Myers argued that the company was denied due process and an opportunity to consult on the regulation.

- *Article 1106, Performance Requirements.* S.D. Myers continued the argument in the *Ethyl* case that any trade ban or prohibition can be a breach of the performance requirements obligation, by requiring an investor to use domestic goods or services.

- *Article 1110, Expropriation.* S.D. Myers argued that the regulation, by depriving them of business opportunities to export PCB waste from Canada to its U.S. facilities, constituted a measure tantamount to expropriation, that required full compensation.

Canada raised two additional important legal issues in its defence. First, it argued that the simple fact of opening offices in Canada does not establish S.D. Myers as an investor with

**Private Rights,
Public Problems:**
A guide to
NAFTA's
controversial
chapter on
investor rights

an investment. This was the first time an arbitral body had to
decide what constitutes an investor or investment under
Chapter 11. Second, Canada also raised issues of compliance
by the NAFTA Parties with two international agreements on
the transboundary movement of hazardous wastes.[7]
Compliance with these agreements is mandatory under their
own terms and is also a recognized requirement in Article 104
of NAFTA.

The "Partial Award" on the merits

The S.D. Myers Tribunal called the decision a Partial Award
because it dealt only with the merits, leaving the damage
award for a second phase. The Tribunal ruled in favour of
S.D. Myers on the national treatment and minimum
international standards grounds, but not on the performance
requirement and expropriation grounds.

What is an investment?

The Tribunal made it clear that what constituted an
investment was a broad concept. It included being in a joint
venture, being a branch of the investor, making a loan to a
related company, and importantly, "its market share in
Canada constituted an investment" (para. 232). This is a
broad reading of the definitions in Chapter 11, Art. 1139.

National treatment

• The Tribunal expressly read into Article 1102 on national
  treatment provisions from elsewhere in NAFTA. These
  included provisions on avoiding the creation of distortions
  to trade, on least trade restrictiveness, and to the effect that
  states had the right to establish their level of
  environmental protection (e.g., para. 247). There is no
  apparent textual basis in Article 1102 for this.

• In defining the critical term of "in like circumstances" the
  Tribunal included the need to avoid trade distortions as a
  factor to consider, thereby again bringing other factors into
  a comparative process.

• The only apparent test it applied was whether the investor
  was in the same sector as Canadian investors it was
  compared to, including "economic sector" or "business
  sector" (para. 250).

• The Tribunal also said that the decision whether two firms
  are "in like circumstances" must take into account
  circumstances that would justify government regulations
  that treat them differently in order to protect the public
  interest. It did not define what these circumstances might
  be (para. 250).

- In looking for different treatment the Tribunal did not compare the treatment of the investor's Canadian broker operation to that received by domestic broker operations. Rather, it compared the investor's integrated operation— including the investor's Canadian broker operation and its U.S.-based disposal facilities—to disposal facilities located in Canada.

- The Tribunal looked to tests of whether the practical effect of a measure was to create a disproportionate benefit for domestic companies; or whether on its face it favoured nationals over non-nationals.

- The Tribunal concluded the measure was discriminatory in intent.

Minimum international standards

- Article 1105 establishes a minimum standard floor of treatment below which treatment of foreign investors may not fall, even if a government is not acting in a discriminatory manner (para. 259).

- "The Tribunal considers that a breach of Article 1105 occurs only when it is shown that an investor has been treated in such an unjust or arbitrary manner that the treatment rises to the level that it is unacceptable from the international level. That determination must be made in the light of the high measure of deference that international law generally extends to the right of domestic authorities to regulate matters within their own borders" (para. 263).

- The breach of the national treatment obligations here also constituted a breach of Article 1105 (para. 266).

Performance requirements

- The Tribunal stated that it must look at the substance of a measure, not its form (para. 273). This meant that a trade measure could also fall within the scope of this prohibition.

- To fall under the prohibitions on performance requirement, a measure must fall squarely within the specific paragraphs that set out the prohibitions. The measure in this case did not fall within these specific prohibitions. (A minority opinion would have held that it did.) (para. 277).

Expropriation

- The Tribunal stated that regulatory action is unlikely to be a legitimate subject of complaint under Article 1110 of

**Private Rights,
Public Problems:**
A guide to
NAFTA's
controversial
chapter on
investor rights

NAFTA, and that the general body of precedent does not treat regulatory action as amounting to expropriation (para. 281).

- However, it goes on to note that a Tribunal must look at the substance of a measure not just its form, and that a regulation could constitute an expropriation (para. 281, 283).

- The Tribunal stated that a key difference between expropriation and regulation is that "expropriations tend to involve the deprivation of ownership rights; regulations a lesser interference" (para. 282). Subsequently, it referred to other factors, such as whether the host country realized any benefit, or whether there was a transfer of property or indirect benefit to others.

- The Tribunal also stated that the purpose and effect of a measure had to be considered, thus creating at least some degree of alternative approach to that seen in Metalclad (para. 285).

- Ultimately, the Tribunal ruled that in this case no expropriation claim could be founded as the measure in question was only temporary and served to delay, but not eliminate a business opportunity (para. 284).

Interpretation of international environmental agreements

- The Tribunal ruled that the language environmentalists had used to argue the primacy of the listed international environmental agreements over NAFTA's trade rules created a condition that requires the application of, *inter alia* the least trade restrictive test and other principles of trade law (para. 215).

- On the interpretation and scope of the *Basel Convention on the Control of Transboundary Movements of Hazardous Wastes and their Disposal* and the *Agreement between the Government of Canada and the Government of the United States of America Concerning the Transboundary Movement of Hazardous Wastes*, both covered by Article 104 of NAFTA, the Tribunal interpreted them, in particular the bilateral agreement, by reading the free trade principles of NAFTA back into both those agreements (paras. 205–216).

- The Tribunal concluded that the Canada-United States Agreement does not authorize one of these two Parties to use its domestic law to bar the import or export of hazardous waste, despite a clause that states the provisions of the agreement are subject to domestic law (para. 208).

Private Rights,
Public Problems:
A guide to
NAFTA's
controversial
chapter on
investor rights

The application for judicial review

On February 8, 2001, Canada filed a Notice of Application for judicial review in the Federal Court of Canada seeking the setting aside of the award in whole or in part.[8] The principle grounds for this are:

- The dispute was outside the scope of Chapter 11 in finding that S.D. Myers was an investor under Chapter 11;

- The interpretation and application of the "in like circumstances" requirement was outside the scope of Chapter 11 by including the operations of the investor in its home state in the scope of comparison;

- The award conflicts with the public policy of Canada by ruling Canada should have allowed exports of PCB wastes in breach of its international obligations.

- The award is wrong in equating a breach of national treatment with a breach of the minimum international standards obligation.

The application had not been scheduled at the time of writing. However, an interesting side issue had arisen as to whether Canada could place the record from the arbitration on the court record, which would make it public. S.D. Myers was objecting to public access to the record if it was filed with the Federal Court of Canada, arguing the confidentiality order of the Tribunal and privacy rules of the arbitration proceeding should continue to apply. This issue was undecided at the time of going to press.

What is the impact of the case?

The *S.D. Myers* case was the first Chapter 11 case to reach a decision on a new environmental measure adopted by a government. It has some very concerning elements, as well as some positive ones.

The broad scope attached to key provisions of Chapter 11 by the Tribunal, engendered in large part by the infusion of trade law principles into the meaning of national treatment and in like circumstances, raises legitimate concerns about how broad Chapter 11 actually is, and is unprecedented in investment or trade law, to the best of the present author's knowledge. This expansion of a simple comparative requirement by reading in trade law principles not found in the provision in question leaves significant uncertainties as to the scope and meaning of this provision.

The recognitions that environmental factors may provide a legitimate basis for finding circumstances to be "unlike" is,

Private Rights,
Public Problems:
A guide to
NAFTA's
controversial
chapter on
investor rights

however, important and should be useful for addressing this issue in later cases. This may be the most important balancing element between investment and environment issues over the longer term.

The determinations on performance requirements and expropriation show significantly more sensitivity to environmental issues on the surface. However, the final disposition of each of these grounds is ultimately cast in narrow terms based in large part on the temporary nature of the measure. This leaves these aspects of the decision open to real ambiguities, and uncertainty in their future application.

One of the more disturbing parts of the judgment from an environmental perspective is the retroactive incorporation of trade principles into the interpretation of the two international environmental agreements discussed, both dealing with the transboundary movement of hazardous wastes. First, it is legally unfounded to interpret two prior agreements, both negotiated in very different contexts and one at a very different level, by infusing them with trade law principles agreed to later in time.

Second, the ruling that the *Canada-United States Agreement on the Transboundary Movement of Hazardous Wastes* does not allow a Party to ban the export or import of such wastes is patently incorrect. Here, one need only contrast the unequivocal supremacy clause in favor of national law in that agreement, which the Tribunal quotes directly, with the highly-conditioned, so-called supremacy clause in Article 104 of NAFTA.[9] The Tribunal's interpretation of Article 104 itself should also shed light on its actual scope and intent, and disabuse early expectations fostered by some that this provision provided a significant additional protection from the application of trade law to the implementation of the listed international environmental agreements. Given the general application of the environmental exceptions found in Article XX of the GATT through its reference in Chapter 20 of NAFTA, the actual impact of Article 104 is called into question by the interpretation of the Tribunal in this case.

Private Rights,
Public Problems:
A guide to
NAFTA's
controversial
chapter on
investor rights

7.

Sun Belt Water Inc. v. Canada

Key dates:

Notice of Intent to Arbitrate: November 27, 1998

Second "Notice of Claim and
Demand for Arbitration":   October 13, 1999

Notice of Arbitration: Not yet filed

The facts

Based on the Notice of Intent to Arbitrate filed by Sun Belt, this potential case concerns a refusal, in 1991, by British Columbia to expand a water export license, and the subsequent suspension of a pre-existing water export license Sun Belt had as part of a Canadian-U.S. joint venture. These licenses were for the bulk export of freshwater from rivers in British Columbia via shipping tankers to the U.S. In 1991, the government of British Columbia imposed a moratorium on all new or expanded licenses of this type, a moratorium that was later made permanent in British Columbia. In 1996, British Columbia settled a claim with the Canadian business partner, but not with the U.S. partner, Sun Belt.

Sun Belt, in the Notice of Intent to Arbitrate, claimed $220 million in damages. This amount was increased to somewhere between $1.5 and $10 billion, including long-term lost profits, in the second Notice of Claim and Demand for Arbitration.

The investor's claims

In the Notice of Intent to Arbitrate, the claim was limited to the allegedly different treatment given the Canadian investor compared to Sun Belt. In the subsequent "Notice of Demand," Sun Belt challenges the underlying right of British Columbia to withdraw the water export permit and ban all water exports. Based on these two documents, the claims appear to include:

- *Article 1102, National Treatment.* Sun Belt claims the differences in the treatment after the license was withdrawn shows preferred treatment for the domestic Canadian partner.

- *Article 1105, Minimum International Standards of Treatment.* Sun Belt argues that a number of different practices alleged to have taken place between it and the government of British Columbia constitute a breach of minimum international standards for treating an investor. This includes the absence of due process and the lack of fair and equitable treatment.

**Private Rights,
Public Problems:**
A guide to
NAFTA's
controversial
chapter on
investor rights

- *Article 1110, Expropriation.* Sun Belt argues that the withdrawal of the license and the imposition of the freshwater export ban was an expropriation under Chapter 11.

What is the impact of the case?

As the case has not formally been pursued to the arbitration stage, it remains in abeyance. Whether it becomes time-barred may be a factor to consider if it is actually initiated into an arbitration proceeding.

The original scope of the case was a traditional comparison of treatment between a domestic and foreign investor. The expanded scope raises questions concerning the ability of a state, province or country to review and revise critical natural resource conservation policies. It also raises questions concerning the definition of freshwater versus containerized water under NAFTA. One of the basic guarantees made by the Parties when NAFTA was signed was that it did not impact domestic freshwater management. Given its suspended state, it is difficult to ascertain what, if any, actual impact this case will have in law, but it did act to galvanize many concerned groups about the potential reach of NAFTA as a whole, and Chapter 11 in particular.

8.
Pope & Talbot Inc. v. Canada

Key dates:

Notice of Intent to Arbitrate:	December 24, 1998
Notice of Arbitration:	March 25, 1999
Interim Award:	June 26, 2000

Case proceeding on two remaining issues

The facts

The case arises from a complicated set of circumstances surrounding ten years of U.S. trade challenges to Canadian softwood lumber exports. These challenges eventually led to the signing of the Canada-U.S. *Softwood Lumber Agreement,* (SLA) which imposed quotas on Canadian softwood exports. Pope & Talbot (P&T), a U.S. company with a subsidiary in British Columbia, claimed its export quotas were cut disproportionately to other exporters, thereby impacting on its profits. (Under the quotas, a certain amount of cut wood could be exported duty free. Above that limit, duty was charged.)

The SLA covered exports from four provinces in Canada (British Columbia, Alberta, Ontario and Quebec). The claimant argued this constituted discrimination as producers in all the provinces were not covered, and argued additionally that they had received less favourable treatment than other companies located in British Columbia.

The investor's claims

The investor argued four separate violations of Chapter 11:

* *Article 1102, National Treatment.* P & T claimed that it was treated differently from producers both in the provinces without a quota and within British Columbia, which had a quota. The company claimed it did not receive the best treatment available in Canada to domestic producers, including in non-quota provinces.

* *Article 1105, Minimum International Standards of Treatment.* P&T argued that the "secretive" way the quotas were applied breached its right to be heard on the quota, to receive reasons for the quotas and to have an appeal of its quota.

* *Article 1106, Performance Requirements.* P&T argued that the quotas on some provinces but not others means that they create an export preference for lumber from non-quota provinces, which acts as a performance requirement. More directly, they argued the quota constituted a maximum allowable export limit.

* *Article 1110, Expropriation.* P&T argued that the loss of ability to sell to its traditional market amounted to an expropriation, or a measure "tantamount to" expropriation, of that part of its business.

The Interim Award

The Tribunal ruled in favour of Canada on the expropriation and performance requirement obligations only, but for interesting reasons. The Tribunal has not yet ruled on the minimum international standards and national treatment issues, arguing that further evidence should be produced and that both should be considered together, thus supplementing the view of other cases as to the relationship between these two obligations. The inclusion of a ruling on only two of the four claims is why the ruling was styled an Interim Award.

Performance requirements
* Article 1106 is to be construed strictly to cover only measures within its seven enumerated requirements (Interim Award, para. 70).

**Private Rights,
Public Problems:**
A guide to
NAFTA's
controversial
chapter on
investor rights

- These prohibitions cover a measure that imposes or enforces any given level or percentage of exports (para. 74). (Note: This reasoning could equally be applied to imports levels of imported product inputs.)

- However, in this case, there was no imposition or enforcement of any specific level of exports. The regime imposed different levels of tariffs on different levels of export, but imposed no limits on the amount of exports. This tariff scheme was not within the scope of Article 1106 (para. 75).

- While the regime deterred increased exports, this did not amount to a requirement or limit (para. 75).

What is an investment?

- Access to the U.S. market for a foreign investor is a property interest subject to protection under Article 1110 on expropriation (para. 96).

- The protection extends to the business of the investment. Interference with that business has an effect on the property that constitutes the investment. In this sense the true interests at stake are the investment's asset base, the value of which here was largely dependent on its export business (para. 98).

Expropriation

- Article 1110 "covers nondiscriminatory regulation that might be said to fall within an exercise of a state's so-called police powers" (para. 96).

- Regulations can be used in a manner that would constitute creeping expropriation. Much expropriation could be conducted by regulation if there were a blanket exception (para. 99).

- The use of the words "measure tantamount to expropriation" does not increase the scope of what international law normally considers to be covered by the concept of expropriation without regard to the magnitude or severity of the effect of the measure (para. 96, 104).

- The Tribunal concluded, however, that the interference with the business activities in this case was not substantial enough to be characterized as expropriation (para. 96).

- The test for expropriation to be applied is one of the degree of interference with the investment.

- The difference between regulation and taking is not always clear but may rest on the degree of interference with the property interest (Footnote 73). "The test is whether that interference is sufficiently restrictive to support a conclusion that the property has been "taken" from the owner" (para. 102).

- Referring to U.S. references, the Tribunal notes that expropriation speaks of an action that is confiscatory, or that prevents, unreasonably interferes with or unduly delays, effective enjoyment of an alien's property (para. 102). Here there was no allegation of nationalization or of a confiscatory regime, with no interference in ownership, day-to-day management, the proceeds of sales, etc. (para. 100).

- The only taking here is the reduced ability to export lumber to the U.S. However, P&T continues to export substantial amounts and earn substantial profits from its ongoing sales to the U.S. (para. 101).

What is the impact of the case?

The inclusion of access to foreign markets as a specifically protected part of an investment expands the idea of protection of foreign investors to include all their trading relationships. This in turn contributes to an expansion of private company rights to use the investor-state process to challenge *trade* measures with an impact on their business, an area of challenge previously reserved only for states.

The ruling on performance requirements also shows the potential for a broad sweep of measures to be covered, as it implies any measure creating an impact on export levels, and by logical extension on imports of product inputs for production, would be covered by this provision, as long as a clear requirement can be found.

The ruling on expropriation is troubling for its singular focus on the significance of the impact of the measure on the investment, the only test apparently applied. The only limiting factor to this may be the specific listings of what this measure was *not*, in particular that it was not a confiscation of the actual ownership or management of the business.

Private Rights,
Public Problems:
A guide to
NAFTA's
controversial
chapter on
investor rights

9.

Methanex Inc. v. United States

Key dates:

Notice of Intent to Arbitrate:	June 15, 1999
Notice of Arbitration:	December 3, 1999
Draft Amended Claim:	February 12, 2001
Hearing on draft amended Claim and on U.S. objections to jurisdictions:	proceeding (June 2001, anticipated)
Petition for *Amicus* Status:	August 26, 2000
Decision of Tribunal on Jurisdiction to accept *amicus* submissions:	January 15, 2001

The facts

Methanex is a Canadian company that manufactures methanol. Methanol is one of the constituent components of MTBE, a gasoline additive. Approximately 40% of Methanex's U.S. sales are used to make MTBE. In March 1999, and after an extensive public consultation and university-led review process, California issued an order that would ban MTBE in all gasoline sold in that state by December 31, 2002. Methanex has argued that the ban would penalize it and MTBE producers for what is really a problem of leaking underground gasoline storage tanks. MTBE is one of the signs, according to Methanex, of gasoline in the groundwater, but the real problem to address is the leaking gasoline tanks. Several other U.S. states have now followed the California lead.

The investor's claims

Methanex claims approximately $1 billion US in damages from the United States. In February, 2001, Methanex sought the permission of the Tribunal to amend its grounds for the claim. (The draft amended claim remains a draft document until the Tribunal accepts it.) The description below indicates what Methanex intends to add to the previous grounds by way of this amendment. The right to amend and other objections to jurisdiction will be heard in June 2001.

- *Article 1102, National Treatment.* This is part of the amended claim, based on assertions that Archer-Daniels-Midland, a competitor that manufactures Ethanol, a product that stands to gain from the MTBE ban, contributed to the campaign of the now Governor of California as part of a successful lobbying effort to achieve the MTBE ban, thereby creating a discriminatory process and outcome. However, Methanex specifically states that it is not asserting that either ADM or the Governor in any way violated U.S. law, but that his judgment lacked fairness and independence because of the political contributions.

- *Article 1105, Minimum International Standards of Treatment.* Methanex argues that the actions banning MTBE resulted from a flawed process in which it was denied due process and a fair hearing, leading to a failure to consider alternatives to banning MTBE. In the draft amended claim, they add two arguments to the grounds claimed for violations of this obligation: (1) the same allegations of unfair and non-transparent lobbying as the determinant of the decision; and (2) that the measure was a disguised restriction on trade and was not the least trade restrictive available. These last grounds are derived directly from trade law.

- *Article 1110, Expropriation.* Methanex claims that the actions taken to ban MTBE go far beyond what was necessary to protect the public interest, failed to consider the legitimate interests of Methanex, and resulted from a failure to enforce other environmental laws. These failures led to a substantial interference and taking of their business and a violation of Article 1110.

The draft amended claim makes specific arguments that environmental regulations are often used as disguised barriers to trade, and are promoted for competitiveness purposes, and uses two previous Chapter 11 cases, *Ethyl v. Canada* and *S.D. Myers v. Canada* as part of its arguments in this regard.

In addition to being presented with these issues, the *Methanex* case also demonstrates two other issues.

Methanex's Citizen Submission under Article 14 of the North American Agreement on Environmental Cooperation

As part of its legal strategy, Methanex filed a submission under Article 14 of the *North American Agreement on Environmental Cooperation*, asking the Secretariat of the Commission for Environmental Cooperation to develop a factual record on whether California is effectively enforcing its environmental laws against leaking gasoline tanks. Methanex claimed if this law were enforced, as well as laws on the performance of small two-stroke motors, then there would be no need to address MTBE. In January, a second Canadian mixer of MTBE initiated a second submission on this same issue.[10] Both of these were reviewed by the Secretariat to see if

**Private Rights,
Public Problems:**
A guide to
NAFTA's
controversial
chapter on
investor rights

they meet initial criteria for acceptance, after which a response from the U.S. government was requested by the Secretariat as part of its procedure on the submissions. However, by the operation of Articles 14(3) and 45(3) of the NAAEC, no factual records can be prepared here because the subject matter is being considered in an international law proceeding, and such duplication is not permitted in the submission process. Both have therefore been terminated. Still, this effort shows how corporations can use international mechanisms to promote their own self-interest.

The Petition for Amicus Status[11]

The Methanex case has already left at least one significant mark on the Chapter 11 landscape. In August, 2000, the International Institute for Sustainable Development, a Canadian NGO, followed by the American NGO EarthJustice in September, 2000, petitioned the Methanex Tribunal for *amicus curiae* status.[12] The underlying basis for this petition was the inherent jurisdiction of the panel to manage its own process.

Methanex filed written submissions opposing the petition, while the United States asked for time to make such submissions. At a procedural meeting on September 7, 2000, the Tribunal asked for further submissions by the two petitioning groups, the litigating Parties, and by Mexico and Canada as Parties to the NAFTA (pursuant to Article 1128 of NAFTA). Throughout this process, Methanex continued to oppose any *amicus* participation, primarily as a breach of the privacy and confidentiality of the arbitration process. Methanex also argued that the Tribunal had no jurisdiction to consider the petition or any actual submissions. Mexico supported the opposition of Methanex to *amicus* participation. However, both the United States, in very extensive submissions, and Canada in a very brief submission, supported the petitions and the jurisdiction of the Tribunal to accept at least written *amicus* briefs.

The decision of the Tribunal on this issue was handed down on January 15, 2001.[13] The Tribunal ruled unequivocally in favor of having the jurisdiction to accept *amicus* briefs in writing, thereby supporting the NGO petitions on this point. It relied primarily on the absence of any specific provisions in either the UNCITRAL Arbitration Rules or NAFTA's Chapter 11 on the possible role of *amici* as the basis for resting its decision on its "broad discretion as to the conduct of this arbitration" under Article 15(1) of the UNCITRAL Arbitration Rules.[14]

While ruling in favor of the petitioners on the legal principle as regards written submissions, the Tribunal rejected the ability to allow oral arguments by *amici* in the absence of the agreement of the litigating Parties. This aspect of the ruling was based on an express provision in the Arbitration Rules requiring hearings to be held in camera unless otherwise agreed by the Parties.[15]

Finally, the Tribunal did not issue an order for the participation of the *amici* in its January decision. Rather, after stating it was "minded" to allow such participation, it stated a final order was premature in light of (1) ongoing issues related to the jurisdiction of the Tribunal, and (2) a concern to hear the disputing Parties on the appropriate procedural modalities for an *amicus* intervention. Consequently, the decision can be seen as a decision in favor of the applicants for *amicus* status, but one that was not yet fully executed.

What is the impact of the case?

The *Methanex* case was the first environment-related case brought against the U.S. by a foreign investor. This has meant a much higher level of public awareness of the issues being raised under Chapter 11 by foreign investors. It also means that all three NAFTA Parties have now seen environmental laws or decisions challenged under Chapter 11.

The claims in the amended claim in effect place American political financing on trial to a large degree. It also foreshadows the most direct debate on the role of trade principles as part of the obligations of Chapter 11. Indeed, the draft amended claim argues that "any violation of an international principle for the protection of trade or investment is also a violation of the NAFTA Article 1105 requirement that state measures be fair, equitable and in accordance with international law." This claim is astonishingly broad, with counsel for Methanex actually arguing the principles are to be included from such extraneous sources as the WTO Agreement on Technical Barriers to Trade.[16] It effectively seeks to expand the scope of Chapter 11 to allow the investor-state process to litigate any trade law issue.

The extensiveness of this approach is supported by counsel based on arguments taken directly from the preceding Chapter 11 cases, as are arguments that market access and market share are protected interests. This highlights the precedential value that is already being attached to the early decisions.

Also at issue is the reach of Chapter 11 to state and provincial laws, where a significant amount of environmental legislation takes place in all three NAFTA countries. The arguments in the draft amended claim reflect the potential suggested by *Metalclad*, that a measure supported by federal law cannot be opposed by other levels of government.

Private Rights,
Public Problems:
A guide to
NAFTA's
controversial
chapter on
investor rights

10.
Ketchum Investments Inc., and Tysa Investments Inc. v. Canada

Key dates:

Notice of Intent to Arbitrate: December 22, 2000

Ongoing

The facts

Ketchum and Tysa are two U.S. companies with controlling shareholder interests in a Canadian forest company called West Fraser Mills, located in British Columbia. The case essentially is similar to the *Pope & Talbot* case against Canada, concerning the distribution of quotas under the *Softwood Lumber Agreement* (SLA) between different companies located in Canada. Like Pope & Talbot, these investors claim their quota has fallen in a manner that is discriminatory both as compared to producers in provinces not covered by the SLA, and as between themselves and other producers within British Columbia.

The investor's claim

The investors claim $30M for violations of all four major Chapter 11 obligations.

- *Article 1102, National treatment*
- *Article 1105, Minimum international standards*
- *Article 1106, Performance requirements*
- *Article 1110, Expropriation*

The Notice of Intent to Arbitrate does not set out further legal basis for these claims.

What are the impacts of the case?

The primary public concern arises from the potential for "copycat" suits under Chapter 11. This case is a direct copy of the *Pope & Talbot* case, commenced after it was made clear by the Tribunal they were going to continue to study the claims in that case under the national treatment and minimum international standards obligations. The investors also maintained the original two grounds already dismissed in the *P&T* case. In the absence of significant fact differences which do not appear to be present from the text of the Notice of Intent, if these grounds are re-opened, it will highlight the uncertainty the current investor-state process has the potential to create for regulators. At present, this action by the investors appears to be a place marker in the event the *P&T* case does succeed.

Private Rights,
Public Problems:
A guide to
NAFTA's
controversial
chapter on
investor rights

11.

Halchette Distribution v. Mexico

Key dates:

Notice of Intent to Arbitrate: 1995

Notice of Arbitration: Not pursued

What was the case about?

There is no publicly available information on this case. What is known is that Halchette is in the airport concession business in Mexico.

The investor's claims

Unknown.

What is the impact of the case?

The case was not pursued. Whether the filing of the Notice of Intent to Arbitrate had any strategic or other impact is not known. It appears that no documents in this case have ever been made public.

12.

Signa S.A. de C.V. v. Canada

Key dates:

Notice of Intent to Arbitrate: 1995

Notice of Arbitration: Not pursued

What was the case about?

There is no publicly available information on this case. Indirect sources indicate that Signa is a Mexican pharmaceutical company with business dealings and other ownership associations with a Canadian pharmaceutical company. The Notice of Intent to Arbitrate coincided with a Canadian regulatory debate on approval of a generic antibiotic.

What were the legal grounds of the case?

Unknown.

What is the impact of the case?

The case was not pursued. Whether the filing of the Notice of Intent to Arbitrate had any strategic or other impact is not known. It appears that no documents in this case have ever been made public.

Private Rights,
Public Problems:
A guide to
NAFTA's
controversial
chapter on
investor rights

13.

Marvin Ray Feldman Karpa (CEMSA) v. Mexico

Key dates:

Notice of Intent to Arbitrate: February 18, 1998

Notice of Arbitration: May 27, 1999

Preliminary decision on jurisdiction: December 6, 2000

Case proceeding

The facts

Feldman is a U.S. national who operates an international trading enterprise, CEMSA, in Mexico. Among other goods, Feldman exported bargain brand cigarettes from Mexico to the United States. He claims that the application of Mexican excise tax rebates for exported cigarettes were applied unequally and that he did not receive the rebates as he should have. He also claims that in December 1997, Mexico reversed its excise tax rebate policy, contrary to law and a Supreme Court decision in Mexico, and an agreed settlement of prior claims on the basis of future rebates, thereby preventing him from receiving the excise tax rebate money he claims he was due, and effectively eliminating his business.

The investor's claims

The Investor claims $50M in damages based on two legal grounds:

- *Article 1105, Minimum International Standards of Treatment.* Feldman claims that the Mexican activities up to and including the reversal of the policy had been designed to prevent him exporting cigarettes and constituted a denial of justice, based on allegations of failure to implement a judicial decision and abandonment of a settlement. The allegations also include a consistent pattern of denial of justice geared to providing Mexican-owned producers a monopoly of export sales of cigarettes.

- *Article 1110, Expropriation.* Feldman claims that the withdrawal of the tax rebate amounts to an expropriation of his business and, therefore, requires compensation. He claims the acts are arbitrary, discriminatory and confiscatory.

Preliminary decision on jurisdiction

This decision was not available to the author at the time of writing.

Private Rights,
Public Problems:
A guide to
NAFTA's
controversial
chapter on
investor rights

What is the impact of the case?

The current information suggests this case is unlikely to have a significant impact on public welfare issues, as it appears to be focused on discriminatory action. However, this cannot be confirmed at present.

14.
Loewen Group Inc. v. United States

Key dates:

Notice of Intent to Arbitrate: July 29, 1998

Notice of Arbitration: October 30, 1998

Decision on Jurisdiction: January 5, 2001

Case proceeding

The facts

Loewen is a Canadian company in the funeral business that entered into some business dealings with American funeral homes and associated enterprises as part of a major expansion program. One set of contracts, valued at $5 million, with the O'Keefe family in Mississippi led to a large court case that was lost at trial by Loewen. The civil trial led to a $500 million US award, which included money for emotional and punitive damages, being entered against Loewen. The punitive damages component was 200 times greater than any punitive damages award ever upheld on appeal. However, in order to appeal, Loewen was required by the courts to post a bond for 125% of the full amount of damages awarded—or $600 million US—which it could not do. Ultimately, Loewen settled the case for $175 million US The investors claim the jury finding and damages award was motivated by continued references to the foreign ownership of the company in the U.S. court proceedings.

The investor's claims

The case focuses on the different treatment Loewen alleges it received in the judicial process compared to what an American defendant would have received as a result of being a Canadian company. It sites numerous instances of alleged bias in this regard. Its grounds focus on three obligations:

• *Article 1102, National Treatment.* In its complaint, Loewen highlights the alleged instances where the legal process was allowed to focus on the nationality of the investor, and where the court accepted "inflammatory" arguments relating to the defendant being Canadian.

**Private Rights,
Public Problems:**
A guide to
NAFTA's
controversial
chapter on
investor rights

- *Article 1105, Minimum International Standards of Treatment.* Using the same issues, Loewen claims that the continued references to the foreign status of the company amounts to a denial of justice and unfair and inequitable treatment. They also claim that the refusal to lower the bond requirement for the appeal, which is often done by the courts, amounted to a denial of the right to appeal.

- *Article 1110, Expropriation.* The final result, and the practical denial of the right to appeal, it is argued, also amounted to an illegal expropriation of the investors assets.

The decision on jurisdiction

What is a measure?

The central point of the U.S. argument that the Tribunal did not have the jurisdiction to hear the case was that the acts of a court were not a "measure" under Chapter 11. All the detailed arguments stemmed from this central point. The Tribunal rejected this argument completely. It ruled that:

- The term "measure" under Chapter 11 had a wide scope, which was inconsistent with the exclusion of judicial acts and decisions (Decision on Jurisdiction, para. 40).

- It is widely accepted in international law that states are responsible for the acts of all branches of government, including the judicial branch (para. 45–47, 70).

The interpretation of NAFTA

On a point of broader interpretational importance, the Tribunal held that:

- NAFTA is not to be understood in accordance with the principle that treaties are to be interpreted in deference to the sovereignty of states (para. 51).

- "The text, context and purpose of Chapter Eleven combine to support a liberal rather than restricted interpretation of the words "measures adopted or maintained by a Party," that is, an interpretation which provides protection and security for the foreign investor and its investment: See *Ethyl Corporation v. Canada* (where the NAFTA Tribunal concluded that the object and purpose of Chapter Eleven is to create effective procedures ….for the resolution of disputes and to increase substantially investment opportunities.(at 83))" (para. 53)

What is the impact of the case?

The *Loewen* case is the first under Chapter 11 to directly challenge the conduct of the judicial system as a breach of

Private Rights,
Public Problems:
A guide to
NAFTA's
controversial
chapter on
investor rights

investment protections. It will, therefore, focus attention on how U.S. courts deal with foreign investors, as well as the ability of federal states in a democracy to impact the judicial process through an international agreement such as this. The decision on jurisdiction that confirms judicial processes and decisions are subject to Chapter 11 obligations suggests the need for this to be appreciated, regardless of the actual outcome of the case on its own specific facts.

15.
Mondev International v. United States of America

Key dates:

Notice of Intent to Arbitrate: May 6, 1999

Notice of Arbitration: September 20, 1999

Case proceeding

The facts

The case concerns the commercial dealings of a Canadian real estate development company in Boston. In particular, the foreign investor argued that it had an option to purchase property from the city of Boston adjacent to property it had already purchased and successfully developed. The value of the property over which the option was alleged to be held had increased substantially due, in part, to the success of the first project. The Chapter 11 case was filed after civil legal proceedings in the state of Massachusetts led to a jury finding in favour of Mondev that was subsequently overturned by the presiding judge in favor of the city of Boston. This reversal by the trial judge was upheld by the Court of Appeal and Mondev was refused leave to appeal to the Supreme Court of the United States.

The investor's claims

The investor claims $50M in damages on grounds that are similar to those in the *Loewen* case:

- *Article 1102, National Treatment.* Mondev argues the constant references to it as a Canadian company, both inside and outside the courts, led to breaches of its national treatment guarantees.

- *Article 1105, Minimum International Standards of Treatment.* Mondev argues that its treatment was below minimum standards of international treatment by being

Private Rights,
Public Problems:
A guide to
NAFTA's
controversial
chapter on
investor rights

arbitrary, by the creation of never before seen
jurisprudence, and by accepting the sovereign immunity
claims of the city, which go beyond what is permitted by
international law.

- *Article 1110, Expropriation.* Mondev argues that the result
of the judicial process was an unlawful taking of its
property, with no valid public purpose (other than money)
and that there was a failure to pay compensation.

What is the impact of the case?

This is the second case to include a challenge of the treatment
of foreign companies and nationals in the U.S. judicial
process. Its legal impact in this context will be viewed in
conjunction with the result in the *Loewen* case.

16.
United Parcel Service v. Canada

Key dates:

Notice of Intent to Arbitrate: January 19, 2000
Notice of Arbitration: April 19, 2000
Ongoing

The facts

United Parcel Service is known the world over as UPS, a leading
courier company that is American owned. UPS' claim is
essentially that it does not receive treatment that is similar to
that received by the package and courier delivery service of
Canada Post, a Canadian crown corporation. UPS argues that
Canada Post uses its monopoly on mail service, including its
distribution capacity and retail services such as sales counters
for stamps and package mailing, to cross-subsidize its courier
service, which is accessible in the same locations and uses the
same infrastructure at least in some respects. UPS also argues
that Canada Post has a superior customs clearance
arrangement in place with Canada Customs and Revenue.

The investor's claim

UPS claims $160M in damages for the following breaches of
NAFTA:

- *Article 1102, National Treatment.* UPS argues that this
obligation is breached because Canada Post does not
provide UPS with access to its retail and service
infrastructure that is equal to what it provides its own

courier operations, as well as in the provision by Canada Customs of a privileged customs clearance arrangement.

- *Article 1105, Minimum standard of treatment.* Canada Post's abuse of its government monopoly to engage in anti-competitive practices towards its competitors in the courier field is argued as a breach of this obligation, as is an alleged lack of transparency in undertaking these same activities.

- In addition, by failing to implement other obligations under NAFTA, UPS argues that Canada itself has breached these obligations and therefore has failed to meet the Chapter 11 obligation to provide a minimum standard of protection. These other obligations include:

  - NAFTA Article 1503 on the effective control of government monopolies; and

  - NAFTA Article 1202, on providing national treatment to service providers and investments in the service sector.

- This last argument, in so far as it relates to Article 1202, calls for a Chapter 11 Tribunal to rule on other external obligations not subject to Chapter 11 through the indirect means of saying all NAFTA, and perhaps other international obligations, are justiciable under the minimum international treatment obligation.

- *Article 1503 of NAFTA.* Article 1116 on the investor-state process allows government obligations under two other provisions to be expressly brought forward as part of a Chapter 11 arbitration. These are Articles 1502(3)(a) and 1503(2). These provisions require the NAFTA Parties to ensure that government monopolies act in a manner that is consistent with all the obligations in NAFTA, including Chapter 11. In essence, these provisions create obligations on the governments to prevent the misuse of a government monopoly vis-à-vis related private sector activities. The claimants invoked these provisions in this case in their own right.

What is the impact of the case?

The monopoly of the postal service is recognized in all states. Here, it is the use of this monopoly that is challenged in so far as it relates to modern services.

What is extremely significant is the use of Article 1105, minimum standards of treatment, to argue that a breach of another international law obligation wholly outside Chapter 11 is covered by it as a breach of minimum international standards. This approach essentially argues that any breach of

Private Rights,
Public Problems:
A guide to
NAFTA's
controversial
chapter on
investor rights

any international agreement can be challenged if it has an impact on a foreign investor. This scope is extremely broad, given the ever-increasing range of international obligations, and would create an unlimited opportunity for private investors to challenge both the implementation and alleged non-implementation of any international obligation. This filing preceded the draft amended claim in the *Methanex* case, which adopts a similar approach.

The treatment of this issue by the Tribunal will be of enormous significance in defining the scope of the Chapter 11 obligations and dispute resolution process. In addition, how Chapter 11 relates to the ongoing operation of government monopolies will be closely watched in this case.

17.

ADF Group v. United States

Key dates:

Notice of Intent to Arbitrate:	February 29, 2000
Notice of Arbitration:	August 25, 2000
Ongoing	

The facts

ADF Group is a Canadian-based company that fabricates and enhances steel products for mega-project construction and other specific construction needs. It has a U.S. facility in Florida as well. In 1999, it entered into a contract with a general contractor to provide specialized steel products and construction services relating to the construction of a major highway interchange in Springfield, Virginia. The construction was subject to the U.S. "Buy America" rules on government procurement, and this was specified in the contract involved. The Buy America rules require, subject to certain exceptions not applicable in this case, that all steel used in government construction projects be produced in America. ADF argued this historically meant that the steel had to be produced in the U.S. but there could be additional processing done to it afterwards outside the U.S. as it did not change the actual steel content itself. It further argued that the steel it used would be American produced, but would only be subject to certain types of additional fabrication work (drilling, milling, etc.) in Canada. This approach was rejected after several meetings by government officials at the federal and state levels, requiring ADF to get the fabrication work done in the U.S. as opposed to its facility in Canada.

Private Rights,
Public Problems:
A guide to
NAFTA's
controversial
chapter on
investor rights

The investor's claim

The investor claims as yet uncertain damages, but of a minimum of $90M, for breaches of:

- *Article 1102, National Treatment.* The Buy America rule, it is argued, provides more favourable treatment to U.S. competitors in breach of this obligation. The inclusion of post-production fabrication for steel under the rule is mentioned separately as well.

- *Article 1105, Minimum standard of treatment.* As this applies to any treatment that is not fair or equitable, not just egregious breaches of fair and equitable treatment requirements, the Buy America program is captured, as it is vague, arbitrary and uncertain and does not permit a fair understanding of the law with sufficient precision. A radical shift by administrative agencies in the interpretation of the law also falls within this obligation.

- *Article 1106, Performance requirements.* ADF alleges that the Buy America rule breaches the prohibition on requiring domestic content for products.

The investor relies also on the general objective in Article 102 of NAFTA, for the Parties to eliminate barriers to trade, facilitate cross-border movement of goods and promote conditions of fair competition.

Note: Chapter 11, Articles 1108(7) and 1108(8), contain specific exceptions for government procurement regulations and policies that are attached to Articles 1102 and 1106 and would appear to be germane to the alleged violation of these obligations. In the Notice of Arbitration, the claimants do not refer to these exceptions, or indicate how they may or may not be relevant to the claim.

What is the impact of the case?

In so far as the case addresses a major aspect of American government procurement policy, and a policy that has considerable public sway at all levels of consumer behavior in the United States, this case will likely achieve a high profile. It demonstrates the ability of Chapter 11 to be used to challenge deeply ingrained programs.

Endnotes

1   *Manganese-based Fuel Additives Act*, S.C. 1997, Ch. 11.

2   *Report of the Article 1704 Panel Concerning a Dispute Between Alberta and Canada Regarding the Manganese-Based Fuel Additives Act,* June 12, 1998, File No. 97/98-15-MMT-P058,

Private Rights, Public Problems:
A guide to
NAFTA's
controversial
chapter on
investor rights

Available at the web site of the Secretariat of the Agreement on Internal Trade, <http://www.intrasec.mb.ca>.

3   News Release: Government of Canada to Act on Agreement on Internal Trade Panel Report on MMT, July 20, 1998, and Government of Canada Statement on MMT, July 20, 1998.

4   In very broad brush terms, a review would allow the Court to set aside all or part of the Tribunal's decision for excess of jurisdiction, but would then usually return the matter to the Tribunal for further consideration. An appeal would allow the Appeal's Court to substitute another decision.

5   *Commercial Arbitration Act, R.S.B.C. 1996 C.55; International Commercial Arbitration Act, R.S.B.C. 1996 C. 233.*

6   See "U.S. Waste Control Firm Refiles Case Under NAFTA Investor-State Provisions," *International Environmental Reporter*, 10-11-2000, p. 791.

7   Canada-U.S. Agreement Concerning the Transboundary Movement of Hazardous Waste, and the multilateral Basel Convention on the Control of Transboundary Movements of Hazardous Wastes.

8   The application is based on the Commercial Arbitration Act, R.S.C. 1985, c. 17 (2nd Supp.)

9   *Ibid*, para. 207, quoting Article 11 of the bilateral Agreement: "The provisions of this Agreement shall be subject to the applicable laws and regulations of the Parties."

10 Methanex Corporation, SEM-99-001, June 1999; NESTE Canada Inc., SEM-00-002. See http://www.cec.org/citizen/guides_registry/index.cfm?varlan=english for the full record of these two submissions.

11 This description is taken from Howard Mann, "NAFTA, Chapter 11, International Environmental Law," Year in Review issue, *The International Lawyer*, Vol. 34, Summer 2001, forthcoming.

12 The Petitions and other documents discussed here can all be found on the IISD web site at http://www.iisd.org/trade/investment_regime.htm. The case carries no formal identification numbers under UNCITRAL Rules. By way of full disclosure, the present author acted as Counsel to the IISD in the proceedings described here.

13 *Methanex Corporation v. United States of America*, Decision of the Tribunal on Petitions From Third Persons to Intervene as "*Amici Curiae*," 15 January, 2001.

14 *Ibid*, para. 26.

15 *Ibid*, paras. 40–42, relying upon Article 25(4) of the UNCITRAL Arbitration Rules.

16 Section III.C.4 of the Draft Amended Claim, February 12, 2001.